Bounded Rationality
in Macroeconomics

ARNE RYDE
8 December 1944–1 April 1968

Bounded Rationality in Macroeconomics

The Arne Ryde Memorial Lectures

THOMAS J. SARGENT

Hoover Institution and University of Chicago

CLARENDON PRESS · OXFORD

Oxford University Press, Walton Street, Oxford OX2 6DP

Oxford New York

Athens Auckland Bangkok Bombay
Calcutta Cape Town Dar es Salaam Delhi
Florence Hong Kong Istanbul Karachi
Kuala Lumpur Madras Madrid Melbourne
Mexico City Nairobi Paris Singapore
Taipei Tokyo Toronto
and associated companies in
Berlin Ibadan

Oxford is a trade mark of Oxford University Press

Published in the United States
by Oxford University Press Inc., New York

© Thomas J. Sargent 1993

Reissued in paperback 1995

British Library Cataloguing in Publication Data
Data available

Library of Congress Cataloging in Publication Data
Data available
ISBN 0–19–828864–6
ISBN 0–19–828869–7 (Pbk)

Printed in Great Britain
on acid-free paper by
Biddles Ltd.
Guildford & King's Lynn

To Bobby,
Nick, and Jon
who can learn at different rates

The Arne Ryde Foundation

ARNE RYDE was an exceptionally promising young student on the doctorate programme at the Department of Economics at the University of Lund. He died after an automobile accident in 1968 when only twenty-three years old. In his memory his parents Valborg Ryde and pharmacist Sven Ryde established the Arne Ryde Foundation for the advancement of research at our department. We are most grateful to them. The Foundation has made possible important activities which our ordinary resources could not have afforded.

In agreement with Valborg and Sven Ryde, we have decided to use the funds made available by the Foundation to finance major initiatives. Since 1973 we have arranged a series of symposia in various fields of theoretical and applied economics. In 1990 we published "Seven Schools of Macroeconomic Thought" by Edmund S. Phelps, the first issue in a series of Arne Ryde Memorial Lectures. The present book by Professor Thomas J. Sargent, based on the lectures he held at Snogeholm Castle in Skane in October 1992, is the second issue in this series. We are very glad and grateful that Professor Sargent agreed to come to Lund to give his Arne Ryde Memorial Lecture.

Bjorn Thalberg

Acknowledgements

This essay served as the text for the Arne Ryde Memorial Lectures which I delivered at Snogeholm Castle near Lund, Sweden, on October 1 and 2, 1992. I thank Professor Bjorn Thalberg for inviting me to give those lectures, and for the hospitality that he and his assistant Jerker Holm showed me during my visit to Lund.

I received very useful comments and criticisms on this essay from Jasmina Arifovic, William Brock, In Koo Cho, John Van Huyck, Charles Goldman, Ramon Marimon, Ellen McGrattan, Rodolfo Manuelli, Carsten Peterson, Harald Uhlig, and François Velde. I thank Albert Marcet, Ramon Marimon, and Ellen Mc-Grattan for our enjoyable collaborations on learning, and for sharing ideas that have helped to shape the views in this essay. My interest in studying economies with 'artificially intelligent' agents was spurred by attending a meeting organized by Kenneth Arrow and Philip Anderson at the Santa Fe Institute in September 1987. I thank Brian Arthur, John Holland, and Richard Palmer for what they taught me at that meeting, some of which is reflected in Chapter 4 of this essay. I thank Jasmina Arifovic, John Hussman, Chung Ming Kuan, Ramon Marimon, John Rust, and Shyam Sunder for sharing their data with me. I thank He Huang for excellent research assistance and for criticizing an earlier version of the manuscript. My research on the subject of learning has been supported by grants from the National Science Foundation.

Maria Bharwada did an excellent job of typesetting this essay in TEX. François Velde provided much valuable help in ingeniously writing Unix and TEX programs to ease the task of manuscript preparation. I am grateful to David Kreps and Darrell Duffie for sharing some TEX macros.

Contents

1
Introduction

Equilibria and transitions

In 1989 the problem of 'transition dynamics' forced itself on economists and statesmen. Two generations of work on economic dynamics within parallel traditions in game theory, macroeconomics, and general equilibrium theory have given us theories of dynamics that have their best chance of applying when people are in recurrent situations that they have experienced often before. In Eastern Europe the transition is not like that: people there are confronted with unprecedented opportunities, new and ill-defined rules, and a daily struggle to determine the 'mechanism' that will eventually govern trade and production. Economists who dispense advice about governmental strategies to enable transitions to a market economy can do so with ample help from 'equilibrium theories' describing how to expect a system to operate after it has fully adjusted to a new and coherent set of rules and expectations, but with virtually no theories about the transition itself. We might have prejudices and anecdotes to guide our preferences among transition strategies, but no empirically confirmed formal theories. [1]

Against this background, more and more economists have recently ventured into what Christopher Sims (1980) characterized as the 'wilderness' of irrational expectations and bounded rationality, aiming partly to create theories of transition dynamics, partly to understand the properties of equilibrium dynamics

---

[1] Fast adjustment or 'cold turkey' advocates say, 'If you want to cut the tail off a dog, don't do it an inch at a time.' Gradualists say, 'If you want to climb a mountain, don't try to do it with a single leap.'

themselves, and partly to create *new* dynamics of systems that do not settle down. Beyond confirming Sims's characterization of this area as a research 'wilderness,' no general theory of transitions or of bounded rationality has yet emerged from this area, but much has been learned, and maybe some of it is relevant to thinking about real transitions.

This essay describes and interprets some of this large and diverse body of work. I do not survey very much of the work in the area, but focus on a small number of examples designed to indicate the kinds of questions that are being asked and answered in this research.[2]

This area is wilderness because the researcher faces so many choices after he decides to forgo the discipline provided by equilibrium theorizing. The commitment to equilibrium theorizing made many choices for him by requiring that people be modelled as optimal decision-makers within a commonly understood environment. When we withdraw the assumption of a commonly understood environment, we have to replace it with *something*, and there are so many plausible possibilities. Ironically, when we economists make the people in our models more 'bounded' in their rationality and more diverse in their understanding of the environment, *we* must be smarter, because our models become larger and more demanding mathematically and econometrically.

Sketch of the argument

The argument in this essay runs as follows. Rational expectations imposes two requirements on economic models: indi-

---

[2] Because of limitations of space in this essay and knowledge in my head, I neglect two large and important related literatures: on learning in games, and on equilibria with Bayesian learning. David Kreps (1990) provides a good introduction to issues about learning in games. Marimon and McGrattan (1993) and Blume and Easley (1992) provide surveys of parts of the literature not treated here. Also see Bray and Kreps (1987), Feldman (1987), Kiefer (1989), Nyarko (1993), Nyarko and Olson (1991), and El-Gamal and Sundaram (1993).

vidual rationality, and mutual consistency of perceptions about the environment. When implemented numerically or econometrically, rational expectations models impute much *more* knowledge to the agents within the model (who use the *equilibrium* probability distributions in evaluating their Euler equations) than is possessed by an econometrician, who faces estimation and inference problems that the agents in the model have somehow solved. I interpret a proposal to build models with 'boundedly rational' agents as a call to retreat from the second piece of rational expectations (mutual consistency of perceptions) by expelling rational agents from our model environments and replacing them with 'artificially intelligent' agents who behave like econometricians. These 'econometricians' theorize, estimate, and adapt in attempting to learn about probability distributions which, under rational expectations, they already know.

To learn how to build models with boundedly rational agents, I turn to the interrelated literatures on statistics, econometrics, and artificial intelligence. These literatures describe methods for representing and estimating relationships within data. I present a broad brush survey of a few bread and butter statistical methods, and describe how they are related to methods developed in the recent 'parallel distributed processing' or neural network literature. I also mention John Holland's genetic algorithm and classifier system and how they compare with least squares methods familiar to economists. It is from the store of methods built up in these literatures that we shall select the 'brains' to give our boundedly rational agents.

Next I shall describe five example economies variously designed to illustrate some of the potential uses and properties of models with boundedly rational agents. Some of these examples illustrate the ability of collections of boundedly rational agents to learn to behave as if they have rational expectations. Other examples illustrate the choices that we the researchers, as the 'gods' or creators of these artificial people, have in informing (or 'hard-wiring') them about their environments before we turn them loose. Still other examples illustrate how putting boundedly rational agents inside some environments can serve to resolve limitations or puzzles (e.g. equilibrium indeterminacy and odd types of behavior) that rational expectations implies in particular models.

Continuing in the spirit of asking what bounded rationality models can do that rational expectations models cannot, I next describe how models with adaptive agents have been used to interpret experiments for two monetary economies. These two economies have serious problems of multiple equilibria under rational expectations, so it is interesting to see how the experimental results compare with the predictions of particular types of bounded rationality.

The argument concludes with an accounting of the promises and limitations for macroeconomics of models with bounded rationality. On the credit side of the ledger are these models' success in inspiring useful tests of equilibrium selection; the motivation they have provided for 'evolutionary programming' for computing equilibria of rational expectations models; and their suggestion, through the literatures on parallel and genetic algorithms, of new gadgets and statistical methods for econometricians. On the debit side (or at least in the to-be-collected row) of the ledger are bounded rationality's unfulfilled promise as a device for specifying and understanding out-of-equilibrium dynamics; and its failure thus far to suggest new and fruitful econometric specifications of expectations formation.

The essay ends near where it started, with a difference between the behavior of econometricians and the agents in their models. As I have interpreted it, the bounded rationality program wants to make the agents in our models more like the econometricians who estimate and use them. Given the compliment ('imitation is the sincerest form of flattery'), we might expect macroeconometricians to rush to implement such models empirically. There has been no rush, maybe for the reason that many macroeconometricians are in the market for methods for *reducing* the number of parameters to explain data, and a reduction is not what bounded rationality promises.

2

Expectations and Behavior

Rational expectations

The idea of rational expectations has two components: first, that each person's behavior can be described as the outcome of maximizing an objective function subject to perceived constraints; and second, that the constraints perceived by everybody in the system are mutually consistent. The first part restricts individual behavior to be optimal according to *some* perceived constraints, while the second imposes consistency of those perceptions across people. In an economic system, the decisions of one person form parts of the constraints upon others, so that consistency, at least implicitly, requires people to be forming beliefs about others' decisions, about their decision processes, and even about their beliefs. [1]

Why have economists embraced the hypothesis of rational expectations? One reason is that, if perceptions of the environment, including perceptions about the behavior of other people, are left unrestricted, then models in which people's behavior depends on their perceptions can produce so many possible outcomes that they are useless as instruments for generating predictions. The combination of its two key aspects – individual rationality and consistency of beliefs – has in many contexts

---

[1] The first use of the term 'rational expectations' that I know is by Hurwicz (1946, p. 133), who did not define the term, but used it in discussing ways of modelling the behavior of a single firm facing an unknown distribution of future output prices. Muth's (1961) definition emphasizes the second aspect of the concept, consistency of perceptions. Hurwicz (1951) used both elements of the concept of rational expectations, though he did not use the term in his discussion of econometric policy evaluation procedures.

made rational expectations a powerful hypothesis for restricting the range of possible outcomes. Another reason for embracing rational expectations is that the consistency condition can be interpreted as describing the outcome of a process in which people have optimally *chosen* their perceptions. That is, if perceptions were not consistent, then there would exist unexploited utility- or profit-generating possibilities within the system. Insisting on the disappearance of all such unexploited possibilities is a feature of all definitions of equilibrium in economics.

Rational expectations (static)

The two components of rational expectations can be illustrated in the context of a static model of a competitive market. There is a large number n of identical firms, each of which chooses its output x to maximize $R(x, p) = p \cdot x - c(x)$, where c is an upward sloping cost function. There is a downward-sloping demand function $p = p(nX)$ expressing price as an inverse function of total output nX in the industry, where X is the output of the 'average' firm in the industry. Each firm takes p as given, i.e. is a 'p-taker' and an 'X-taker,' and chooses x to maximize $R(x, p)$, which means setting x to satisfy the condition 'price equals marginal cost', i.e. $p = c'(x)$. Denote the solution to this problem by $x^* = \text{argmax}_x R(x, p) = g(p)$, where 'argmax' means the maximizing value of x. Since $p = p(nX)$ via the market demand function, we can also write $x = g(p(nX)) = h(X)$. The first component of rational expectations thus induces a 'best-response' mapping $x = h(X)$ from a given average (or 'aggregate') setting for X to an optimizing individual choice of x.

The second component of rational expectations imposes consistency between individuals' choices and what their perceptions are of aggregate choices. Because in this simple setting all firms have been assumed identical, imposing consistency amounts to requiring that $X = h(X)$, so that each firm ends up choosing what it assumes as a p-taker (and as an X-taker) that the average firm is choosing. By requiring that $x = X = h(X)$, we are insisting that each firm, when it acts competitively, has no incentive to deviate from the average setting for x that others are assuming in solving their optimum problems.

Thus, a static rational expectations equilibrium is the usual model of a competitive market.

Rational expectations (dynamic)

In the static context just described, a rational expectations equilibrium is a fixed point of the 'best response mapping' $h(X)$, a fixed point being a positive real number.[2] However, we often want to study dynamic situations in which individuals choose not one-time actions, but entire sequences of actions. In dynamic contexts, we formulate a rational expectations equilibrium as a fixed point in a space of sequences of prices and quantities, or, equivalently, a fixed point in a space of *functions* that determine sequences of prices and quantities. We need to define a dynamic analogue of the static best response mapping h.[3] This will turn out to be a mapping from a perceived law of motion for the model's endogenous state variables to an actual law of motion.

Let x be a state variable for an individual, for example a stock of capital or labor, and let X be the average value of that same state variable over a large number of identical agents, each of whom chooses a *contingency plan* or *decision rule* $x_t = h(x_{t-1}, X_{t-1}, u_t)$ to maximize

$$(1) \qquad E \sum_{t=0}^{\infty} \beta^t R(x_t, x_{t-1}, p_t)$$

subject to

$$(2) \qquad \begin{aligned} p_t &= p(X_t, u_t) \\ X_t &= H(X_{t-1}, u_t) \end{aligned}$$

---

[2] Or, in random models, a random variable.

[3] The example in this section is close to that of Lucas and Prescott (1971).

where $\{u_t\}$ is an independently and identically distributed random sequence, $\beta \in (0,1)$ is a discount factor, and $E(\cdot)$ is the mathematical expectations operator. The second equation of (2) is a perceived law of motion or 'forecasting equation' for the aggregate state X_t, while the first equation of (2) is an equation for forecasting market price conditional on the value of X_t. The individual solves this problem, taking X_{-1} and x_{-1} as given. The *Euler equation* for the maximization of (1) with respect to (2) is

$$R_1(x_t, x_{t-1}, p_t) + \beta \int R_2(x_{t+1}, x_t, p_{t+1}) dF(p_{t+1}|X_t) = 0,$$

where R_i is the partial derivative of R with respect to its ith argument and $F(\cdot|X_t)$ is the cumulative distribution function of p_{t+1} conditional on aggregate X_t that is induced by the pair of equations (2).[4]

A function $h(x_{t-1}, X_{t-1}, u_t)$ that solves this problem is itself a *functional* of the functions R and H and the discount factor β. The solution of the firms's optimization problem, $x_t = h(x_{t-1}, X_{t-1}, u_t)$, implies that the actual law of motion of the aggregate state is given by $X_t = h(X_{t-1}, X_{t-1}, u_t) \equiv H^*(X_{t-1}, u_t)$. In this way, substituting the condition that the representative firm is representative ($x_t = X_t$) into the solution of the firm's optimum problem determines the actual law of motion $H^*(X_{t-1}, u_t)$ when the perceived law of motion is $H(X_{t-1}, u_t)$. So optimizing behavior and representativeness of the representative firm induce a mapping

$$H^* = T(H),$$

[4] Another condition for maximization is the transversality condition

$$\lim_{t \to \infty} E_0 \beta^t R_1(x_t, x_{t-1}, p_t) = 0,$$

where $E_0(\cdot)$ is the expectation conditional on X_0 with respect to the distribution of p_t induced by (2).

from a *perceived* law of motion to the *actual* one. A rational expectations equilibrium is a fixed point of the mapping T:

$$H = T(H).$$

Within a rational expectations equilibrium, firms are solving their Euler equation using the *equilibrium* conditional distribution $F(p_{t+1}|X_t)$, that is, the distribution of prices that is induced by (2) with the equilibrium H. The two key features of a rational expectations equilibrium are captured by saying that the firm determines its decision by solving an Euler equation (this is the individual optimization part of the definition) using the distribution F for the endogenous variable, p_t, that is induced by market clearing and the optimizing behavior of others in the market (this is the consistency of perceptions postulate).

A model of money and prices

These ideas can be illustrated with a rational expectations version of the 'quantity theory' about the relationship between prices and the money supply. We use a non-random version of the theory.

We generate a demand for money by assuming that a representative household or money-holder chooses its level of nominal balances m_t to carry over from time t to time $t + 1$ to maximize the objective function

$$\ln(2w_1 - m_t/p_t) + \ln(2w_2 + m_t/p_{t+1}^*),$$

where we assume that $w_1 > w_2 \geq 0$. Here $2w_1 > 0$ is a parameter that measures resources now available to consume or save in the form of real balances, while w_2 is a parameter that measures resources that will become available next period. The objective function describes how the money-holder weighs the sacrifice involved in holding m_t units of currency this period, which costs him $1/p_t$ units of goods for each dollar held from this period to the next, against the additional $1/p_{t+1}^*$ units of goods that he expects this dollar will command next period. The money-holder chooses m_t, taking as given the current price level p_t and what he expects the price level will be next period, p_{t+1}^*. The maximizing choice of m_t determines the money demand function[5]

$$(3) \qquad m_t/p_t = w_1 - w_2 p_{t+1}^*/p_t.$$

To make (3) operational requires a theory of how the expectation p_{t+1}^* is formed. We can build in rational expectations as follows. Suppose that the supply of money is exogenously set by the government to follow the law of motion

$$(4) \qquad M_{t+1} = \mu M_t$$

for all time t. Suppose further that the household observes the money supply at t, and that it believes that the price level is related to the money supply via the relationship

$$(5) \qquad p_t = \gamma M_t + \lambda^t c,$$

where (γ, λ, c) are constants that summarize the household's expectations or beliefs. We assume that these parameters take values for which the price level is always positive for any positive money supply for any time $t \geq 0$. In particular, we assume that $\gamma > 0, c \geq 0, \lambda \geq 0$. Suppose also that the household knows the value of μ in the law of motion for the money supply, and that it uses the law of motion for the money supply and equation (5) to forecast the price level next period as

$$p_{t+1}^* = \gamma \mu M_t + \lambda^{t+1} c.$$

---

[5] This is a version of the demand function for money used by Phillip Cagan (1956) to study hyperinflations. The objective function that we have attributed to the household corresponds to one that is often used in versions of Paul Samuelson's (1958) overlapping generations model; for example, see Neil Wallace (1980).

Substituting this equation into (3) and (5) and rearranging gives

(6) $m_t = \gamma(w_1 - w_2\mu)M_t + \lambda^t(w_1 - w_2\lambda)c.$

Equation (6) shows a common feature of models in which expectations about the future play a role: the *demand* for money can be regarded as depending on the *supply*. This dependence emerges because current demand depends on expectations about future price levels, and future price levels are believed to depend on future values of the money supply, which are related to the current money supply by the law of motion (4). Equation (6) determines the demand for money as a function of exogenous variables known at t, namely, the money supply.

To compute a rational expectations equilibrium, we set the demand equal to the supply, $m_t = M_t$ in (4), and solve the resulting 'functional equation':

$$M_t = \gamma(w_1 - w_2\mu)M_t + \lambda^t(w_1 - w_2\lambda)c.$$

This equation has a function of M_t on both the right and left sides. We have a rational expectations equilibrium if these two functions are equal, which occurs only under the conditions

(7)
$$\gamma = (w_1 - \mu w_2)^{-1}$$
$$\lambda = w_1/w_2.$$

When the parameters assume these values, the price level obeys the law

(8) $p_t = (w_1 - \mu w_2)^{-1}M_t + (w_1/w_2)^t c.$

When prices follow this process, the household's expectations about the price level are given by $p^*_{t+1} = \gamma\mu M_t + \lambda^{t+1}c$, and always turn out to be correct. Notice how the parameter μ from the law of motion of the money supply enters the equation (8) which shows how the price level depends on the money supply.

The equilibrium is not unique. For any constant $c \geq 0$ we have an equilibrium. Since $w_1/w_2 \geq 1$, for any equilibrium with $c > 0$, prices have a component that is unrelated to money supply behavior and that is growing exponentially at rate w_1/w_2. There is one equilibrium (the one with $c = 0$) in which the price level is proportional to the money supply. All of the (continuum of) other equilibria have the price level rising in what is referred to as a purely speculative 'bubble.'[6] This is one among many examples in which rational expectations equilibria are not unique, in which case 'fundamentals' are incapable by themselves of determining market prices and quantities.[7]

Extending back to Ricardo and Wicksell, there is a tradition in macroeconomics of using models with indeterminate equilibria to criticize the arrangements or operating procedures that the modeller shows to cause the indeterminacy. We turn briefly to an indeterminacy that has haunted international monetary theory.

Another indeterminacy

We can adapt the above model of money and prices to describe an indeterminacy in a theory of exchange rates in a world of fiat currencies.[8] We now assume that (1) governs the *total* demand for two currencies, which are available in total supplies M_{1t} and M_{2t}, respectively, at time t. We also assume that the two currencies are perfect substitutes so long as their rates of return

---

[6] Blanchard and Watson (1982) have pointed out that there are many other equilibria of a stochastic version of this model, formed by regarding p_{t+1}^* as the mathematical expectation of p_{t+1} conditioned on information known at time t. These equilibria are identical to (8) except that now c in (8) is replaced by a stochastic process c_t, where $\{c_t\}$ is any martingale.

[7] In computing a rational expectations equilibrium, we are solving for the parameters γ, λ, c that determine people's beliefs (through (5)) as functions of other parameters in the model. When an equilibrium is *unique*, 'beliefs' contribute *no* free parameters to the model. When equilibria are not unique, as in this example, some of the free parameters index beliefs.

[8] Versions of this result are due to Russell Boyer (1971) and Kareken and Wallace (1981).

are equal. The supplies are governed by the laws of motion

(9)
$$M_{1t+1} = \mu_1 M_{1t}$$
$$M_{2t+1} = \mu_2 M_{2t}.$$

Let p_{jt} be the price level denominated in units of currency j, $j = 1, 2$. Let p^*_{jt+1} be the expected price level in units of currency j. We suppose that the two currencies are always expected to appreciate at the same rate, so that

(10)
$$p^*_{1t+1}/p_{1t} = p^*_{2t+1}/p_{2t},$$

a condition that makes holders of currency indifferent about which currency they hold. (People's indifference about the composition of their money holdings will be the key feature rendering the exchange rate indeterminate.)

Suppose that people believe that the price levels p_{1t}, p_{2t} are determined by

(11)
$$p_{1t} = \gamma_1 M_{1t} + \gamma_2 e M_{2t} + c\lambda^t$$
$$p_{2t} = e^{-1} p_{1t},$$

where e is a *constant* exchange rate. Equations (9), (10), and (11) imply that forecasts of the price levels are made according to

(12)
$$p^*_{1t+1} = \gamma_1 \mu_1 M_{1t} + \gamma_2 e \mu_2 M_{2t} + \lambda^{t+1} c$$
$$p^*_{2t+1} = e^{-1} p^*_{1t+1}.$$

Notice that (11) and (12) imply that (10) is satisfied and is expected to remain satisfied. Substituting these into the demand for money, denominated in units of currency 1, namely, $m_t/p_{1t} = w_1 - w_2 p^*_{1t+1}/p_{1t}$, gives

$$m_t = \gamma_1(w_1 - \mu_1 w_2)M_{1t} + \gamma_2(w_1 - \mu_2 w_2)e M_{2t} + c\lambda^t(w_1 - w_2\lambda).$$

For equilibrium, we require that $m_t = M_{1t} + e M_{2t}$; i.e., the demand for currency denominated in units of currency 1 equals the total supply. This determines a functional equation,

$$M_{1t} + e M_{2t} = \gamma_1(w_1 - \mu_1 w_2)M_{1t} + \gamma_2(w_1 - \mu_2 w_2)e M_{2t} + c\lambda^t(w_1 - w_2\lambda),$$

whose solution is

(13)
$$\gamma_1 = (w_1 - \mu_1 w_2)^{-1}$$
$$\gamma_2 = (w_1 - \mu_2 w_2)^{-1}$$
$$\lambda = w_1/w_2$$
$$c \geq 0 \qquad e \in [0, +\infty).$$

These equations are remarkable because they leave the exchange rate e unrestricted. If these equations have a solution for *one* $e \in (0, \infty)$, then they have a solution for any other $\hat{e} \in [0, \infty)$. Furthermore, the formulas for γ_1, γ_2 do not involve the exchange rate e.

Besides being of substantive interest, such models of monies, prices, and exchange rates provide examples of some important methodological issues involving the construction and application of rational expectations models. First, notice how an equilibrium was constructed by using a 'guess and verify' or 'undetermined coefficients' method. In each example, we guessed at an expectations-generating function of a particular form (linear) with free coefficients, and then computed the values that those coefficients would have to take if expectations were to be rational in light of the structure of the complete model. This solution procedure is silent about how the agents being modelled are supposed to have acquired the beliefs attributed to them. Furthermore, this solution procedure works only in very special cases (essentially only in linear models). In more general settings, the model builder needs some other method for finding an equilibrium.

Second, these are examples of a class of rational expectations models in which equilibria are not unique. There are multiple systems of beliefs, indexed by the parameter c in the money model and by the parameter pair (c, e) in the exchange rate model, that are consistent with rational expectations. Rational expectations alone is not a sufficiently restrictive principle to determine outcomes. If we want to apply such a model to interpret economic time series, some principle other than rational expectations must be used to choose among the possible equilibrium outcomes.[9],[10]

Computation and 'stability' of equilibrium

Static stability and 'adaptive expectations'

We are confronted with the following two distinct but, in practice, related questions. First, given the parameters of a model, how might an equilibrium actually be computed by economists interested in applying the model; and second, supposing that the market 'starts' from some non-equilibrium quantity X^*, can we describe an 'adjustment mechanism' that under particular circumstances would eventually converge to equilibrium?

For our static model, a starting point for many computational schemes is the following 'relaxation algorithm':

(14) $$X_k^* = X_{k-1}^* + \lambda(X_k - X_{k-1}^*)$$

or

$$X_k^* = X_{k-1}^* + \lambda(h(X_{k-1}^*) - X_{k-1}^*),$$

where $\lambda \in [0,1]$ is a so-called 'relaxation parameter,' and X_k^* is the estimate of the equilibrium value at the kth iteration. For some assumptions about the best response mapping h, there

---

[9] King, Wallace, and Weber (1992) build a model in which many stochastic paths of exchange rates are equilibria.

[10] In a class of overlapping-generations models with free currency substitution, Manuelli and Peck (1990) show that the only restriction that equilibrium imposes on the exchange rate is that it conform to a bounded martingale. They construct various types of equilibria, some depending on long histories of 'fundamentals' that are used in effect to synthesize innovations used to drive martingale exchange rate fluctuations. In the Manuelli–Peck context, it is hard to imagine exchange rate fluctuations that are 'too volatile' either in the sense that they are inconsistent with equilibrium or in the sense that their volatility reflects (Pareto) bad welfare outcomes.

exists a $\lambda \in (0, 1)$ for which this scheme converges to the equilibrium value $X = h(X)$.[11]

In this iterative scheme, X_k^* can be loosely interpreted as an 'expected' or 'anticipated' value[12] of X at iteration k, while $X_k = h(X_{k-1}^*)$ is taken to be the 'actual' value at iteration k. Each iteration of the scheme adjusts the expected value towards the actual value by an amount determined by λ. 'Stability' has sometimes been taken to be the requirement that such a scheme converges.

Suitably reinterpreted, this iterative scheme provides a basis for Friedman's and Cagan's concept of 'adaptive expectations.'[13],[14] The equilibrium of the static model describes a timeless situation, or else a situation in which nothing changes with the passage of time. One motivation behind the idea of 'adaptive expectations' was to 'tack dynamics' onto a static model by replacing iteration step k by calendar time t, and to take the resulting equation as a description of how agents form expectations about X from one period of time t to the next. With k replaced by t, equation (14) can be rearranged into the equivalent forms

$$X_t^* = (1 - \lambda)X_{t-1}^* + \lambda X_t,$$

or

(15) $$X_t^* = \lambda \sum_{j=0}^{\infty} (1 - \lambda)^j X_{t-j},$$

[11] One set of sufficient conditions amounts to requiring that an associated differential equation $(d/dt)X = h(X) - X$ have a unique rest point and that it be stable about it.

[12] In a loose 'psychological' sense, not in the sense of mathematical expectation.

[13] 'Adaptive' mechanisms will be described throughout this book. At this point, the phrase just refers to schemes of the form (14) in which an estimate of an object is adjusted in a direction to diminish the discrepancy between it and the object. By varying the 'space' in which the object under study resides and sometimes also by making λ a decreasing function of the iteration number k, many different adaptive mechanisms will have representations like (14).

[14] Milton Friedman credits A. W. Phillips as having suggested the adaptive expectations formulation to him.

which are two alternative forms of adaptive expectations. In their studies of hyperinflation and consumption, respectively, Cagan and Friedman used their adaptive expectations scheme to describe the evolution of people's expectations in real time. In their studies, the expectations-generating function (15) played a key role in determining system dynamics. Their work showed that using (15) with $\lambda \in (0,1)$ helped them to fit and to interpret the data in terms of dynamics largely driven by expectations formation. Cagan and Friedman left open the question of why people would choose to form expectations according to (15).[15] Friedman and Cagan took λ to be a free parameter of their models, the single free parameter describing beliefs.

John F. Muth wanted to eliminate λ as a free parameter. Muth sought simple *dynamic* environments in which it would be a good idea to form expectations as in (15). He structured his search as an 'inverse optimal prediction' problem, seeking a univariate stochastic process for X_t with the property that the linear least squares forecast of X for at least some horizon would be of the form (15). He found that (15) would be the optimal forecast of X_{t+k} over *any* horizon k if and only if X_t evolved according to a univariate stochastic process described by

$$(16) \qquad X_t = X_{t-1} + \epsilon_t - \lambda \epsilon_{t-1},$$

where ϵ_t is a martingale difference sequence. This is the only environment for which the forecasting scheme (15) delivers unimprovable forecasts, given the information that the rule uses. In Muth's vision, the forecasting scheme (15) inherits its one parameter λ from the stochastic process (16) actually governing the $\{X_t\}$ process being forecast.[16] Muth's work was the first application of the idea of rational expectations to find restrictions

[15] Friedman took up the question later (Friedman 1963).
[16] In the context of Cagan's (1956) model, Sargent and Wallace (1973), Christiano (1987), and Hansen and Sargent (1983) studied multivariate versions of Muth's inverse optimal prediction problem, and found joint processes for money and prices that make optimal an adaptive expectations scheme for forecasting prices. For the permanent income example studied by Muth, Sargent (1987, ch.

across a forecasting scheme and an economic–statistical environment in which that scheme was to be used; it led subsequent researchers[17] to think of the forecasting scheme itself as the object in terms of which the equilibrium of a dynamic model is to be defined.[18]

Computation of dynamic equilibrium

In moving from our static example to the dynamic one, we did something quite different from simply tacking the Cagan–Friedman adaptive expectations scheme onto the static model: we changed the *space* of objects in terms of which we defined an equilibrium. Whereas in the static model the equilibrium was defined as a real number representing the quantity of output in the industry, in the dynamic model the equilibrium was defined as a *function* mapping past values of industry output and random disturbances into future values of industry output. In effect, we defined the equilibrium in terms of an expectations-

---

XIII) provides a different solution of the inverse optimal predictor problem that rationalizes Friedman's specification.

[17] See Lucas and Prescott (1971) and Brock (1972).

[18] Muth wanted to deduce restrictions on expectational distributed lag models of the general form

$$x^*_{t+1} = a(L)x_t,$$

where x^*_{t+1} is interpreted as a forcast of x_{t+1} conditioned on observations through t, and $a(L)$ is the polynomial in the lag operator $a(L) = a_0 + a_1 L + \ldots a_n L^n$. In effect, Muth proposed restricting $a(L)$ to be the systematic part of an autoregressive representation of x_{t+1}. Grandmont (1990) has formalized and extended a pre-Muthian set of restrictions on $a(L)$. He proposes that for a fixed set of frequencies $\omega \in [0, \pi]$, the forecasting scheme should be able perfectly to forecast periodic sequences $x_t = \cos(\omega t)$. This leads to the restrictions

$$\cos(\omega_j) = (a(\exp(i\omega_j)) + a(\exp(-i\omega_j)))/2,$$

for the frequencies ω_j chosen. Imposing these restrictions at $n + 1$ frequencies determines $a(L)$. (For example, for frequency $\omega = 0$, the restriction is $a(1) = 1$, which is the famous 'sum of the weights equals unity' restriction.) Early work in the rational expectations literature (e.g. Lucas 1972; Sargent 1971) described the conflict between this way of restricting distributed lags and Muth's.

generating scheme that is *optimal* given the economic environment.

The adaptive expectation scheme (15) is a particular example of a *distributed lag* expectations scheme that maps a history $X^t = (X_t, X_{t-1}, \ldots,)$ into an anticipated value of X. Muth's (1960) purpose was to find a particular stochastic environment H^* expressing X_{t+1} as a function of the history X^t and additional random factors $\{u_t\}$,

$$(17) \qquad\qquad X_t = H^*(X^{t-1}, u_t),$$

and for which Cagan and Friedman's scheme would be an 'optimal' distributed lag. Normally, we are in an opposite situation to the one Muth studied: we start from a description of the environment, and want to find an H^* function that is 'self-generating.' ·

One way to think about computing equilibrium in a dynamic model is to consider iterations mapping estimates of the function H^* into new estimates. Corresponding to (14), we have the adaptive scheme

$$H_k^* = H_{k-1}^* + \lambda(H_k - H_{k-1}^*)$$

or

$$(18) \qquad H_k^* = H_{k-1}^* + \lambda(T(H_{k-1}^*) - H_{k-1}^*),$$

where $\lambda \in (0, 1]$ is again a relaxation parameter. Equation (18) is a scheme for revising entire (expectations-generating) functions in response to discrepancies between their predictions and actual outcomes. We shall meet such schemes again.

Bounded rationality

Behavioral aspects of rational expectations

The idea of rational expectations is sometimes explained informally by saying that it reflects a process in which individuals are inspecting and altering their own forecasting records in ways to eliminate systematic forecast errors. It is also sometimes said to embody the idea that economists and the agents they are modelling should be placed on an equal footing: the agents in the model should be able to forecast and profit-maximize and utility-maximize as well as the economist – or should we say the econometrician – who constructed the model. These ways of explaining things are suggestive, but misleading, because they make rational expectations sound less restrictive and more behavioral in its foundations than it really is. It was not the way that Muth originally defined rational expectations, and it misses key features of the way rational expectations models are implemented in practice.

Rational expectations equilibrium as a fixed point in a mapping from perceived to actual laws of motion typically imputes to the people inside the model much *more* knowledge about the system they are operating in than is available to the economist or econometrician who is using the model to try to understand their behavior. In particular, an econometrician faces the problem of *estimating* probability distributions and laws of motion that the agents in the model are assumed to know. Further, the formal estimation and inference procedures of rational expectations econometrics assume that the agents in the model already know many of the objects that the econometrician is estimating.

Artificial agents who act like econometricians

Herbert Simon and other advocates of 'bounded rationality' propose to create a theories with behavioral foundations by eliminating the asymmetry that rational expectations builds in between the agents in the model and the econometrician who is estimating it. The idea of bounded rationality might be implemented by requiring that the agents in the model be more like the econometrician in one or more of several ways. The agents might be like 'classical econometricians,' who are sure of their model but unsure of parameter values; they might be like 'Bayesian econometricians,' who are unsure of their models and parameter values but can say how they are unsure; or they might be like many practicing macroeconomists, who are unsure even about whether they want to proceed as if they are classical or Bayesian econometricians.

We can interpret the idea of bounded rationality broadly as a research program to build models populated by agents who behave like working economists or econometricians. To lay out the road ahead, it will be useful to say a little more about what we mean by 'behave like economists.'

Practice of economics

Like any science, economics has these parts: a body of *theories* (self-contained mathematical models of artificial worlds); methods for collecting or producing *data* (more or less error-ridden and disorganized measurements); statistical methods for comparing a theory with some measurements; and a set of informal procedures for revising theories in the light of discrepancies between them and the data.[19] The intent of the 'bounded rationality' program is to work the methodology of science doubly hard because, in attempting to understand how collections of people who make decisions under uncertainty will interact, it will use models that are populated by artificial people who behave like working scientists.[20] These artificial people process data and make decisions by forming and using theories about the world in which they live. In other words, the economist

[19] In economics, procedures for revising theories in light of data are typically informal, diverse, and implicit.
[20] Primo Levi said 'a chemist does not think, indeed does not live, without models ...' (*The Periodic Table*: Levi 1984, p. 76)

will assume that he is modelling sets of people whose behavior is determined by the same principles that he is using to model them.[21]   *Rational expectations* is an equilibrium concept that at best describes how such a system might eventually behave if the system will ever settle down to a situation in which all of the agents have solved their 'scientific problems.'

Partly because it focuses on outcomes and does not pretend to have behavioral content, the hypothesis of rational expectations has proved to be a powerful tool for making precise statements about complicated dynamic economic systems. In game theory and general equilibrium theory, we have learned how to impose the two hypotheses of individual rationality and consistency of beliefs in more and more varied and interesting contexts.

The idea of building dynamic theories with behavioral foundations by modelling agents as economists or scientists is intuitively attractive and consistent with the way many of us see the world. But implementing this vision has proved difficult for a variety of reasons, a paramount one being that we don't really have a tight enough theory or description of how economists or other scientists learn about the world. And within economics and other sciences, there are important differences in how different practitioners go about the process of discovery.

Artificial intelligence

Thus, an impediment to implementing bounded rationality as a viable research program is the wilderness of possibilities into which it seems to lead us. Precisely how are we to go about building models populated by agents who in some sense are behaving 'like us scientists'? A number of economists are answering this question by combing the recent literature on artificial intelligence as a source of methods and insights. The past

[21] Such a system can contain intriguing self-referential loops, especially from the standpoint of macroeconomic advisors, who confront the prospect that they are participants in the system that they are modelling at least if they believe that their advice is likely to be convincing.

fifteen or so years has seen an explosion of work designed to create artifical systems or 'brains' that adapt and learn. Some of these methods embody sensible versions of at least aspects of what we might mean by 'behave like a scientist.' The process of borrowing methods from this literature to create economic models has already led to a variety of models of bounded rationality. The remainder of this book will be devoted to surveying parts of the literature on artificial intelligence and to describing how they are related to methods that macroeconomists might already know and use or might eventually come to use.

Questions and payoffs

In the methodology of positive economics of Milton Friedman (1953), economic models are judged by how the outcomes that they predict match data measuring the economy. From the standpoint of this methodology, the behavioral emptiness of rational expectations is neither virtue nor defect.[22] To justify the research effort called forth by the bounded rationality program, we require some prospective payoffs in terms of concrete questions that rational expectations models are not likely to be capable of answering. What are these questions, and where are the likely payoffs?[23]

---

[22] Niels Bohr said, 'It is wrong to think that the task of physics is to find out how nature is. Physics concerns what we can *say* about nature.' This quotation is from the biography of Bohr by Abraham Pais (1992).

[23] I exclude from the following list of potential payoffs the aim of building psychologically deeper or 'more realistic' models of the way people behave. The cognitive psychologist Lawrence Barsalou (1992, p. 9) points out that 'Cognitive constructs – as I will call internal constructs in cognitive psychology – typically do *not* represent conscious mental states. Instead, they typically represent unconscious information processing.' To the extent that we think that economic decision-makers are acting consciously, Barsalou warns us not to expect too much help from his field at the present time.

Equilibrium selection

Rational expectations models sometimes have too many equilibria.[24] When there are multiple equilibria, it means that the physical description of the economy together with the notion of equilibrium are not sufficient to pin down a unique predicted outcome. Many rational expectations models have unique equilibria, but enough of them have multiple equilibria that researchers in game theory and general equilibrium theory have turned to models of bounded rationality somehow to reduce the multiplicity of equilibria. In these contexts, the motivation for embracing a behavioral theory of out-of-equilibrium behavior is the hope that, by studying plausible processes of adapting to out-of-equilibrium behavior, we will find that only particular types of equilibria are possible limit-points of out-of-equilibrium behavior. We shall encounter several more or less successful examples of work motivated in this way.

New sources of dynamics

While rational expectations has proved to be a powerful method of generating rich and interesting dynamics in various contexts, there are particular areas in which the outcomes that it predicts are sharp but very difficult to reconcile with observations. A leading example is from finance, where a powerful 'no trade' theorem characterizes a class of situations in which diversely informed traders are so efficiently extracting information from equilibrium prices that literally no volume of trade can occur in any equilibrium. To explain volume data from financial markets, one needs a model for which the no-trade theorem fails to hold. For rational expectations models, it has proved very difficult to produce a compelling rational expectations model that breaks the no-trade theorem. This has led researchers such as Princeton's Harald Uhlig and Stanford's John Hussman to be-

---

[24] David Kreps (1990) discusses issues involving equilibrium selection in games. Many of the issues in this essay, and some of the viewpoints, are identical to ones discussed by Kreps in related contexts.

gin studying models of asset markets populated by boundedly rational differentially informed agents.

This is but one example of a class in which it seems that sticking with rational expectations might not give us enough flexibility to model all of the dynamics in the data, and in which resorting to adaptive models may help us. Even in macroeconomics within the rational expectations tradition, models are routinely used in ways that are inconsistent with rational expectations.

Analyses of 'regime changes'

Rational expectations models have been used to make statements about the consequence of *regime changes*, a term that is often used in a way that precludes its being consistent with rational expectations. I have in mind work that characterizes a government policy rule as an arbitrarily given state- and time-contingent policy rule, then computes a rational expectations equilibrium under two different such policy rules. Often the first rule is a 'pre-reform' rule meant to describe the government's behavior historically, while the second rule is what the modeller intends as an improved rule. The change in outcomes across hypothetical economies operating for ever under these different rules is then used to predict what would occur if the proposed government policy rule were to be adopted at some future date.

This way of generating predictions is inconsistent with rational expectations because, by comparing equilibria of *different* economies, it predicts what would happen if at some time in the future the government were to deviate from what it had initially been assumed to have for ever committed itself to.[25]

---

[25] A modeller can solve a *Ramsey problem* by finding the government policy rule that, within a class, optimizes an objective function that the modeller attributes to the government, typically a weighted average of the utilities of the agents in the model. In this work, *commitment* by the government is modelled formally as selecting a state- and time-contingent policy rule at time 0, and then never reconsidering any decision. Using models to compute *Ramsey policies* is consistent with rational expectations, at least under this particular assumption about

Under rational expectations, if the government was to have had the option of changing its behavior at future points in time, the agents in the model should have been given the opportunity to take this possibility into account. That is, if the government were really choosing *sequentially* and not once-and-for-all at time 0, under rational expectations the response of 'the market' would change in ways that depend precisely on the government's motives and the dates at which it is given the opportunity to choose. Under a thorough application of rational expectations, if the government really has the option to default from its time 0 plan, that option should be described and the initial equilibrium recomputed under a set of beliefs for private agents about how likely it is that the government will choose that option.

Despite the fact that they are inconsistent with rational expectations, these types of *regime change* experiments have been a principal use of rational expectations models in macroeconomics. One example is the analysis of the ends of hyperinflations in terms of monetary and fiscal policy 'regimes.'[26] To analyze the ends of hyperinflations, models of money like the one described above have been used to compute rational expectations equilibria under two alternative full-commitment monetary–fiscal regimes. A first, 'pre-reform,' regime has permanent large government net-of-interest deficits that are permanently financed by high rates of printing government-issued currency. A second, post-reform, regime has a government budget that is permanently balanced in present value, and no currency is ever created to finance government deficits. These models predict permanently high rates of inflation in the first regime, and no inflation in the second regime.

the *timing* of government decisions, because it builds in optimizing behavior on the part of all agents and imposes a consistent set of expectations across agents.
[26] The description in the text fits my own work on the ends of big hyperinflations (Sargent 1986, ch. 3), but misses some influential analyses of hyperinflations. Flood and Garber (1983) and LaHaye (1985) have focused on the effects during the hyperinflation of speculation about when a stabilization will occur. Also, see Hamilton's (1989) model of regime switches.

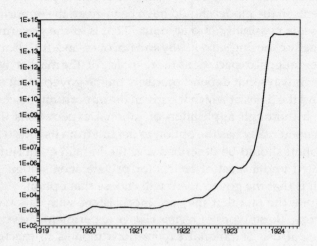

Figure 1. Wholesale Prices in Germany, 1919–1924

This comparison has been used to interpret data like Figures 1 and 2, which show the abrupt stabilizations of price levels at the ends of hyperinflations in Germany and Austria after World War I. In each country, the end of the hyperinflation coincided with a set of government actions that seem consistent with implementing a switch from the first regime to the second regime that I have just described. That the price stabilizations occurred so rapidly perhaps provides some reason for thinking that we don't make much of an error by ignoring the possibility that the prospects of a regime change occurring should really have been built in when analyzing the initial regime.

Retreating from rational expectations

The hyperinflation example is one in which not insisting on consistency with rational expectations is justified as a short-cut

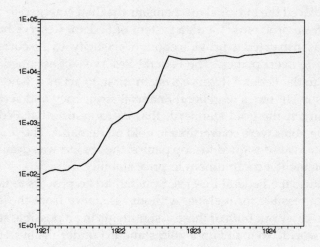

Figure 2. Retail Prices in Austria, 1921–1924

that, for the question at hand, appears to cost little. There is another class of historical examples in which giving up on rational expectations at some (shrewdly chosen) point seems essential for understanding what is going on. Understanding the arrangements and disturbances that led to the onset of the Great Depression is a case in point.[27] I shall describe two competing stories about the onset of the Great Depression, each of which uses many elements of rational expectations, but essential to each of which is a backing off of rational expectations at some level.

Here is the first story. For fifteen years after its inauguration in 1914, the Federal Reserve System was widely regarded as having solved the problem of financial fragility that had been mani-

---

[27] The very speculative remarks in this section are based on recollections of discussions at the Federal Reserve Bank of Minneapolis with Neil Wallace.

fested earlier in recurrent panics and temporary suspensions of convertibility of banks' deposits into gold. The Federal Reserve Act replaced the informal mechanisms that had emerged to cope with those problems[28] with a system of Federal Reserve banks that was instructed to provide enough 'elasticity' to the currency supply to avert panics. The Federal Reserve Act assigned two duties to the Federal Reserve System: first, to act as a 'lender of last resort' in times of general financial stringency and second, to maintain the gold standard, that is, to assure that Federal Reserve notes were convertible to gold on demand. The first assignment was designed to stop panics; the second was designed to implement a commitment to price stability.

Because the Federal Reserve System had no powers to tax, it was not feasible for it alone, without assistance from the Treasury, to carry out both of these assignments in all possible states of the world. To maintain a gold standard under the system of fractional gold reserves then in place, the government had to stand ready to tax enough to 'service' the debt that it had issued or insured, in this case in the form of Federal Reserve notes and liabilities convertible into them. If it had no powers to tax, or to induce other agencies to tax to support its assignments, the central bank could assure convertibility into gold only by running a version of a 100 percent reserves policy. This would entail preventing banks and other financial institutions from intermediating risky private indebtedness in exchange for notes and deposits that claimed to be convertible into gold. In that way, the Federal Reserve could have maintained the convertibility of its own notes, although in doing so it would resign its duty to maintain an elastic currency and so give up functioning as a lender of last resort for banks who were in the business of intermediating risky liabilities.

If it had been relieved of the assignment to maintain convertibility into gold, it would have been feasible for the Federal Reserve to act as a lender of last resort, by appropriately man-

---

[28] See Friedman and Schwartz (1963, pp. 156–68).

aging timely depreciations of the currency against gold.[29] In effect, relieving the Federal Reserve of the assignment to maintain convertibility with gold would have given it a tax (the 'inflation tax') with which to finance its lender-of-last-resort (or bailout) activities.

So it was not feasible for the Federal Reserve to carry out these two assignments. Nevertheless, during the 1920s many people talked and acted as though they believed that the Federal Reserve could and would carry out those assignments; and for a string of years the system seemed to be working. Too many bankers and depositors regarded the system as sound, and failed to recognize that the scheme was infeasible in some states of the world. Instead, bankers and depositors responded as though they were operating under a form of unpriced implicit deposit insurance (for what else does 'lender of last resort' mean?) and they responded appropriately. Operating in their shareholders' interests, banks undertook riskier projects than they would have in the absence of implicit deposit insurance, thereby exposing the system to increased risk and bringing closer the day when the Federal Reserve might be called upon to lend in such volume as to jeopardize its commitment to the gold standard. That situation arose in 1931, when the banks and depositors learned that it was not feasible for the Federal Reserve both to act as a lender of last resort and also to keep the system on gold. Until 1933, when Roosevelt engineered a big depreciation in terms of gold, the Federal Reserve met its gold standard commitment at the expense of its lender-of-last resort function. Banks' and depositors' failure fully to 'see through' the Federal Reserve System's infeasible promises set in motion a process that led to massive financial failure.

Notice how this story uses bits and pieces of rational expectations reasoning, but suspends rational expectations beyond a point. The story has people 'look several steps ahead,'[30] but has

---

[29] See Beers, Sargent, and Wallace (1983).

[30] Thus, the banks are assumed to understand the workings of a 'Modigliani–

them stop well short of seeing through the entire mechanism.

There is an alternative story, which backs off from rational expectations in perhaps a more obvious way than does the first one. Written into the Federal Reserve Act was a version of the 'real bills doctrine,' according to which the Federal Reserve banks were instructed freely to discount at low interest rates high-quality (i.e. relatively risk-free or 'real') evidences of commercial indebtedness as a device to provide an 'elastic currency.' The sense of the 'real bills' policy was to integrate money and credit markets, by making the supply of currency depend on the state of credit markets. There is evidence that during the 1920s the Federal Reserve System was operating under a version of a real bills regime.

The real bills regime has long been criticized by advocates of an alternative set of rules for running a central bank which can be described as a 'quantity theory' regime. The quantity theory regime aims to separate the money market from the credit markets, in order to prevent fluctuations in the supply and demand for credit from impinging on the price level. Because borrowers are cut off from currency holders as potential lenders, under a quantity theory regime there is typically less elasticity of the currency supply and a higher level of interest rates than under a real bills regime.[31] The levels of equilibrium interest rates and asset prices depend on the monetary and intermediary-regulation regime in place.

Here, then, is our second story. During the 1920s the Federal Reserve ran a real bills regime, which participants in the economy assumed was a full-commitment, everlasting policy regime. But starting around 1930,[32] the Federal Reserve abruptly

Miller theorem,' which describes the incentives that the system seems to have given them for increasing the risk in their portfolios to the benefit of their shareholders. See Kareken and Wallace (1978) and Merton (1978). But the banks, investors, and creators of the Federal Reserve are assumed not to foresee (or care about?) the system-wide consequences of their behaviors.

[31] See Sargent and Wallace (1982) and Bruce Smith (1988) for comparisons of the quantity theory and real bills regimes.

[32] Perhaps partly due to the death of Benjamin Strong.

began to administer a quantity theory regime. This entailed an upward movement of real interest rates, causing all sorts of assets to suffer capital losses, and turning many 'good loans' into 'bad loans.'

The structure of our second story shares with our hyperinflation example the key feature that the prime mover is an exogenous change in government policy. However, in the present story, it is essential that the government's change in policy and its consequences were not anticipated beforehand.

These stories should not be confused with hard analyses, and are intended only to indicate how using rational expectations models in 'impure' ways that do not fully impose the two key features of rational expectations (individual rationality and consistent expectations) provides ample – maybe too much – freedom to explain some observations that are difficult to explain if if we remain thoroughly faithful to rational expectations.

New optimization and estimation methods

There is another lode of likely benefits from studying the artificial intelligence literature, but these have less to do with finding new ways of modelling the adaptive behavior of economic agents and more to do with finding new ways of conducting our own business as economists. As practicing economists, we are always on the lookout for new ways of solving optimization, estimation, and numerical analysis problems. The literatures on artificial intelligence and neural computing are full of ideas that are potentially applicable to our problems as researchers. In the spirit of the bounded rationality research program, which is really to put the economist and the agents in his model on an equal behavioral footing, we expect that, in searching these literatures for ways to model our agents, we shall find ways to improve ourselves.

Plan of the book

The elementary object of analysis in rational expectations models and models of bounded rationality is a collection of *decision rules*, namely, functions mapping people's information into decisions. Rational expectations restricts those decision rules by adopting the two assumptions of individual optimization and consistency of perceptions. Bounded rationality drops at least the second of these assumptions, and replaces it with heuristic algorithms for representing and updating decision rules. Students of bounded rationality are therefore in the market for good ways of encoding decision rules and updating them as new information flows in.

The next two chapters briefly survey the two spots where researchers have gone prospecting for the algorithms needed to populate models with boundedly rational artificial agents. The first place is an old literature on statistics and econometrics, while the second is a newer literature on networks and artificial intelligence.

After surveying some of these methods and describing their relationships in Chapters 3 and 4, in Chapter 5 we put some of the methods to work on five examples. Then Chapter 6 describes two laboratory experiments that have been performed on versions of one-currency and two-currency versions of the model of money and prices described above; the authors of both of these experiments used adaptive algorithms to interpret their results. Chapter 7 sums things up.

3
Data Structures

Statistics and bounded rationality

Statistics studies methods of making inferences and decisions when we aren't sure what is happening. For economists, statistics has long been the place to go prospecting for hypotheses to understand how people behave under conditions of uncertainty and ignorance. It must be our starting place, because we propose to make our agents even more like statisticians or econometricians than they are in rational expectations models.

The purpose of this chapter is to review the workings of that centerpiece of econometrics, least squares regression, and how in many contexts it can be implemented recursively. This review will set the stage for the following chapter on neural networks and artificial intelligence, material that is less familiar to most economists, but which we shall see just implements recursive least squares in various ingenious contexts. In this chapter and the next we shall be looking for devices to hand over to the boundedly rational agents that will be created in Chapter 5.

Representation and estimation

From statistics, economists have borrowed and adapted a set of methods for describing and interpreting relationships within data sets. The task of description has fruitfully been subdivided into two logically distinct but interrelated pieces: *representation* and *estimation*. *Representation* of a relationship means positing a mathematical model that is assumed to have generated the data.

Usually, the data are taken to be a random sample drawn from a particular probability distribution, and the task of representation is to select a tractable model describing that probability distribution, typically in terms of a small number of parameters. The mathematical model chosen to represent the data is sometimes called the 'data generating mechanism.' The job of representation is 'purely mathematical' and in itself involves no use of statistical inference. Statistical methods are used to *estimate* the free parameters of the mathematical model, on the basis of the data set under study.[1]

This chapter briefly describes some of the data-generating mechanisms that economists widely use, and also the sorts of procedures that they use to estimate the parameters of those models. My purpose is to convey the flavor of these data-generating mechanisms and statistical procedures, and to set the stage for our subsequent comparisons with neural networks.

Two versions of the linear regression model

Population version

Linear regression, a pillar of econometrics, is a tool for summarizing the linear structure of a vector of random variables. We have a probability distribution function $F(y_t, x_t)$ for (y_t, x_t) where y_t is a scalar and x_t is a $k \times 1$ vector. We assume that the probability distribution has well defined first and second moments. We want to represent the probability distribution in the form

$$y_t = \beta' x_t + e_t,$$

where $\beta' x_t$ approximates y_t in the sense that $e_t = y_t - \beta' x_t$ is as small as possible in the mean square norm $E e_t^2$, where E is the

---

[1] A third aspect of data interpretation is the study of the quality of *approximation*, in which an analyst studies the behavior of some estimates that would be appropriate under the assumption that model A is correct when in truth model B has actually generated the data set. Sims (1972), White (1982), and Hansen and Sargent (1993) have studied the issue of approximation in various contexts.

mathematical expectation. The object is to select β to minimize $V(\beta) \equiv 0.5\, Ee_t^2 = 0.5E(y_t - \beta' x_t)^2$.

The first-order condition for minimization of $V(\beta)$ is $V'(\beta) = 0$, where $V'(\beta) = Ex_t(y_t - x'\beta)$. Thus, the (population) least squares β satisfies the *orthogonality condition*

$$\text{(1)} \qquad\qquad Ex_t(y_t - x_t'\beta) = 0,$$

or

$$\text{(2)} \qquad\qquad \beta = (Ex_t x_t')^{-1} Ex_t y_t.$$

Notice that the population least squares regression coefficients is a mathematical object defined in terms of the population second moments of the distribution $F(y_t, x_t)$. By virtue of the orthogonality condition (1), because $e_t = y_t - x_t'\beta$, the least squares regression represents y_t as the sum of linear function of x_t and a piece e_t that is orthogonal to $\beta' x_t$.

The sample version

We have a sample of observations $\{y_t, x_t\}_{t=1}^T$ drawn from the distribution $F(y_t, x_t)$. Everything that we know about the moments of $F(y_t, x_t)$ is contained in the sample $\{y_t, x_t\}_{t=1}^T$. From these data, we want to estimate the unknown value of β in the model

$$y_t = \beta' x_t + e_t.$$

We can accomplish this by replacing expectations with sample means in formula (2); namely, we use

$$\text{(3)} \qquad \beta_T = \left(\frac{1}{T} \sum_{t=1}^{T} x_t x_t' \right)^{-1} \left(\frac{1}{T} \sum_{t=1}^{T} x_t y_t \right).$$

This is 'ordinary least squares.'

Vector autoregressions

Following the advice of Sims (1980), macroeconomists often use systems of linear regressions, with one equation for each variable being studied, to represent the dynamics within a collection of economic time series. Each variable is regressed against lagged values of itself and all of the other variables in the model.

Let z_t be an $(n \times 1)$ covariance stationary stochastic process (i.e., one for which the vector of means Ez_t is independent of time and the matrix covariances $C_z(k) = Ez_t z'_{t-k}$ are well defined and independent of calendar time t). For convenience, assume that $Ez_t = 0$. Under particular conditions, such a process has the *autoregressive representation*

$$z_t = \sum_{j=1}^{\infty} A_j z_{t-j} + \epsilon_t,$$

where ϵ_t is an $(n \times 1)$ vector of least squares residuals or 'innovations' that satisfies the extensive orthogonality conditions

$$E\epsilon_t z'_{t-j} = 0_n, \quad j = 1, \ldots, \infty.$$

This model is called a *vector autoregression*. The force of the extensive orthogonality conditions in the last equation is to decompose z_t into a piece $\sum_{j=1}^{\infty} A_j z_{t-j}$, which is linearly predictable from past values of the vector process itself, and a part ϵ_t, which cannot be predicted linearly from past z_s's (i.e., it is orthogonal to each element of past z_s's). The matrices of autoregressive coefficients A_j are determined by the normal equations

$$C_z(k) = \sum_{j=1}^{\infty} A_j C_z(k - j), \quad k \geq 1$$

which are equivalent with the least squares orthogonality conditions.

The vector autoregressive representation is a workhorse. Following the lead of Sims and Litterman, it is often used to represent systems of interrelated time series for the purposes of describing their dynamic structure and forecasting them. In constructing our models of economic agents, economists often describe their beliefs about the dynamics of the environment in terms of a vector autoregression. We use vector autoregressions to formulate our own forecasting problems, and often model economic actors as doing the same.

Estimation of vector autoregressions

If enough data were available, vector autoregressions could be well estimated by applying ordinary least squares, equation by equation. But economists usually don't have enough data to use ordinary least squares, so Sims and Litterman have shown how to use modified versions of least squares. I postpone discussing why in practice they deviate from using ordinary least squares in its unadulterated form.

Stochastic approximation

Robbins and Monro (1951) considered the problem of finding a value of a vector α that solves the equation

$$(4) \qquad E\,Q(z_t,\, \alpha) = 0,$$

where Q is a function that is decreasing in α, and $\{z_t\}$ is a sequence of vectors of random variables z_t drawn from some sequence of probability distributions $F_t(z^t)$ where $z^t = \{z_t,\, z_{t-1}, \ldots, z_0\}$. It is assumed that

(a) either a sample $\{z_t\}_{t=1}^{\infty}$ has been generated by 'nature,' or one can be generated by simulation; or

(b) the function $Q(z_t,\, \alpha)$ can be evaluated for the generated z_t and any admissible candidate α.

The stochastic approximation algorithm for computing a sequence of estimates α_t of the value α^* that solves (4) is

$$(5) \qquad \alpha_t = \alpha_{t-1} + \gamma_t \, Q\,(z_t, \alpha_{t-1})$$

where $\{\gamma_t\}$ is a nonincreasing sequence of positive numbers satisfying

$$(6) \qquad \lim_{t \to \infty} t\,\gamma_t = 1.$$

Robbins and Monro (1951) and their followers described conditions under which

$$(7) \qquad \lim_{t \to \infty} \alpha_t = \alpha^*,$$

where α^* solves either $EQ(z_t, \alpha^*) = 0$ (in the case that $\{z_t\}$ is drawn from a distribution that is stationary) or $\lim_{t \to \infty} EQ (z_t, \alpha^*) = 0$ (in the case that $\{z_t\}$ is asymptotically stationary).

It has been discovered that the limiting behavior of a sequence $\{\alpha_t\}$ determined by stochastic difference equation (5) is described by an associated differential equation,

$$(8) \qquad \frac{d}{d\tau}\,\alpha = E\,Q(z, \alpha_\tau),$$

where $E\,Q(z, \alpha)$ is the expected value of $Q(z_t, \alpha)$, evaluated with respect to the asymptotic stationary distribution of $\{z_t\}$.[2]

A heuristic justification for (8) notes that for large values of t algorithm (5) is approximated by

$$\frac{d}{dt}\alpha \approx \frac{\alpha_t - \alpha_{t-1}}{1} \approx \frac{1}{t}EQ((z, \alpha_{t-1})),$$

---

[2] Lennart Ljung (1977) and Ljung and Söderström (1983) have written extensively about the connection between stochastic approximation algorithms and some associated ordinary differential equations. Among economists, M. Aoki (1974) was one of the first to show the applicability of the stochastic approximation algorithm to study learning. See Ljung, Pflug, and Walk (1992) for a description of recent developments.

where replacing $Q(z_t, \alpha_{t-1})$ in (5) with an expected value at a fixed α, namely, $E(Q(z, \alpha))$, is justified by observing that, for large t, $\alpha_t \approx \alpha_{t-1}$, and that the randomness in z will make its variation large relative to the variation in α_t. Use the time transformation $\tau(t) = \log(t)$ to write this differential equation as

$$\frac{d}{d\tau} \alpha_\tau \approx EQ(z, \alpha),$$

which is the ordinary differential equation (8) to be used to approximate the limiting behavior of α_t in (5).

A recursive formulation of the least squares estimate of the mean $Ez_t = \mu$ provides a simple example of stochastic approximation. The least squares estimate is the sample mean $\bar{z}_t = (1/t) \sum_{s=1}^{t} z_s$. Subtracting the sample mean at $t - 1$ from both sides of this formula and rearranging gives

$$\bar{z}_t = \bar{z}_{t-1} + (1/t)(z_t - \bar{z}_{t-1}),$$

which is in the form of (5) with the 'gain' $\gamma_t = 1/t$. The usual initial condition for this equation is $\bar{z}_0 = 0$.[3],[4]

Recursive least squares

The stochastic approximation algorithm can be used to implement the least squares formulas recursively. Suppose that we set $z_t = (y_t, x_t)$, $\alpha = (\beta, R)$, $\gamma_t = 1/t$, and

$$(9) \qquad Q(z_t, \alpha) = \begin{cases} R^{-1} x_t(y_t - x_t'\beta) \\ x_t x_t' - R. \end{cases}$$

---

[3] Prior information about the mean can be represented by using an initial condition other than 0.

[4] For this estimator, the associated differential equation is

$$d/dt\, \bar{z} = \mu - \bar{z},$$

whose solution is $\bar{z}(t) = \mu + \exp(-t)(\bar{z}(0) - \mu)$, which converges to μ for any initial value $\bar{z}(0)$.

Then the stochastic approximation scheme becomes

(10)
$$\beta_t = \beta_{t-1} + \gamma_t R_t^{-1} x_t (y_t - x_t' \beta_{t-1})$$
$$R_t = R_{t-1} + \gamma_t (x_t x_t' - R_{t-1}) .$$

Starting from appropriate initial conditions (β_0, R_0), this is a method for calculating (3). Alternatively, it can be interpreted as a Bayesian procedure for updating estimates starting from a prior distribution $\mathcal{N}(\beta_0, R_0)$.

Least squares as stochastic Newton procedures

Sometimes we want to minimize the function $V(\theta)$ with respect to θ. The *gradient descent method* is iteratively to choose θ_k according to

(11)
$$\theta_k = \theta_{k-1} - \gamma_k V'(\theta_{k-1})$$

for some positive step-size sequence $\{\gamma_k\}$. *Newton's method* is to choose $\{\theta_k\}$ according to

(12)
$$\theta_k = \theta_{k-1} - \gamma_k V''(\theta_{k-1})^{-1} V'(\theta_{k-1}).$$

For the regression problem, we choose $\theta = \beta$ and $V(\beta) = 0.5 E(y_t - \beta' x_t)^2$. Since $V'(\beta) = -E x_t (y_t - x_t' \beta)$ and $V''(\beta) = E x_t x_t'$, a gradient descent and Newton's method become, respectively,

(13) $$\beta_k = \beta_{k-1} + \gamma_k E(x_t y_t - x_t x_t' \beta_{k-1})$$
(14) $$\beta_k = \beta_{k-1} + \gamma_k E(x_t x_t')^{-1} E(x_t y_t - x_t x_t' \beta_{k-1}).$$

Notice that, with $\gamma_k \equiv 1$ for all k, Newton's method converges in one step to the population least squares vector β given by (2).

A comparison of the population formula (1) with the recursive least squares formula (10) motivates the interpretation of (10) as a *stochastic Newton algorithm*.

Nonlinear least squares

Suppose that we want to fit the *nonlinear regression* model

$$y_t = g(x_t, \beta) + \epsilon_t,$$

using the sample $\{y_t, x_t\}_{t=1}^T$. In population, our problem is to choose β to minimize

$$V(\beta) = 0.5E(y_t - g(x_t, \beta))^2 = 0.5E\epsilon_t(\beta)^2$$

where $\epsilon_t(\beta) = y_t - g(x_t, \beta)$. In this problem, the least squares orthogonality condition is

$$(15) \qquad E\psi_t(\beta)\epsilon_t(\beta) = 0,$$

where $\psi_t(\beta) \equiv \nabla\epsilon_t(\beta)$ is the gradient of $\epsilon_t(\beta)$ with respect to β.

Various recursive algorithms are designed to find solutions of (15). Stochastic gradient algorithms iterate on

$$(16) \qquad \beta_t = \beta_{t-1} + \gamma_t \psi_t(\beta_{t-1})\epsilon_t(\beta_{t-1}).$$

Stochastic Newton algorithms iterate on versions of

$$(17) \qquad \begin{aligned} \beta_t &= \beta_{t-1} + \gamma_t R_t^{-1}\psi_t(\beta_{t-1})\,\epsilon_t(\beta_{t-1}) \\ R_t &= R_{t-1} + \gamma_t(\psi_t(\beta_{t-1})\psi_t(\beta_{t-1})' - R_{t-1}). \end{aligned}$$

Unlike the linear case, for nonlinear regressions these algorithms are not equivalent with corresponding 'off-line' algorithms.[5],[6]

---

[5] Kuan and White (1991) show that the recursive estimators are root-T consistent and share the asymptotic distribution of (non-recursive) nonlinear least squares.

[6] In the estimation literature, 'on-line' algorithms refer to estimators that have the *recursive* structure of, for example, stochastic approximation algorithms, the estimator at t being represented as a function of the estimator at $t - 1$ and the data observed at t. 'Off-line' estimators have the property that the estimator at t cannot be expressed in this way; instead, the estimator at t must be written as a function of the entire sample of observations up to time t.

Classification

Classification with known moments

Following Fisher (1936), least squares regression can be used to find a *linear discriminant function* for determining to which of two predetermined classes an individual belongs.[7] We are given two populations, $x_1 \in X_1$ and $x_2 \in X_2$, of $k \times 1$ random vectors, each with common covariance matrix V, but with different mean vectors $Ex_1 = \mu_1, Ex_2 = \mu_2$. Vectors x will be drawn from a mixture of the two distributions, with equal probability. Our task is to find a rule for *classifying* an x that is randomly drawn from this mixture of populations X_1 and X_2, i.e., we want to say whether x is from X_1 or from X_2. Note that the classification into X_1 and X_2 is given. For now, we assume that the means μ_1 and μ_2 and the common covariance matrix V are known.

A solution of this problem is attained with the *linear discriminant function*. We want to find a linear function $\beta'x - \beta_0$, where β is a $k \times 1$ vector and β_0 is a scalar, so that our decisions can be made according to the rule

(18)   if $\beta'x - \beta_0 \geq 0$, then x is a member of X_1;

          if $\beta'x - \beta_0 < 0$, then x is a member of X_2.

For a given variance of the random variable $\beta'x$, which equals $\beta'V\beta$ and can be interpreted as 'variance within a population,' we want to choose β to separate the two populations as much as possible. Discrepancy betweeen the two populations is to be measured by the criterion $\beta'(\mu_1 - \mu_2)$. Our goal is to choose β to maximize $\beta'(\mu_1 - \mu_2)$, subject to $\beta'V\beta = c$, where $c > 0$ is a constant. The maximizing value of β is

$$\beta = \lambda^{-1}V^{-1}(\mu_1 - \mu_2),$$

---

[7] See Kendall (1957).

where λ is a Lagrange multiplier on the constraint, which can be set equal to one (which amounts to a choice of the variance c in the constraint).

For a sample equally likely to be drawn from populations X_1 and X_2, the expected value $E\beta'x$ is $\beta'(\mu_1 + \mu_2)/2$. For the discriminant function, we therefore choose β_0 in (18) according to $\beta_0 = \beta'(\mu_1 + \mu_2)/2$.

When X_1 and X_2 are each multivariate normal, the discriminant function (18) has an interpretation in terms of a likelihood ratio test. This is because the log likelihood ratio can be represented as

$$x'V^{-1}(\mu_1 - \mu_2) - 0.5(\mu_1 + \mu_2)V^{-1}(\mu_1 - \mu_2),$$

so that (18) can be read as stating that x should be assigned to population X_1 whenever the likelihood ratio exceeds one (or the log likelihood ratio exceeds zero).[8]

Estimated parameters

When the means (μ_1, μ_2) and covariance matrix V are not known *a priori*, they are estimated by sample means and co-variances, where the sample covariance is estimated by pooling observations across the X_1 and X_2 populations. Sample estimates are substituted into (19) to obtain the sample discriminant function.

Fisher (1936) showed that the linear discriminant function can be derived by a regression on dummy variables on x. For a sample of $k \times 1$ vectors x_t, where observations for $t = 1, \ldots, N_1$ are drawn from population X_1 and observations $t = N_1 + 1, \ldots, N_1 + N_2$ from population X_2, define $y_t = \frac{N_2}{N_1 + N_2}$ for $t = 1, \ldots, N_1$, $y_t = -\frac{N_1}{N_1 + N_2}$ for $t = N_1 + 1, \ldots, N_1 + N_2$. Then the estimated linear discriminant function can be obtained from an ordinary least squares regression of y_t on x_t for this sample.

[8] See Anderson (1958).

Principal components analysis

Population theory

Let x_t again be a $k \times 1$ random vector with second moment matrix $V = Ex_t x_t'$. The method of *principal components* analysis is based on the eigenvector decomposition of V, namely, $V = PDP^{-1}$, where P is an orthogonal matrix whose columns are eigenvectors of V, and D is the corresponding diagonal matrix of eigenvalues of V. This decomposition of V induces a transformation of the $k \times 1$ vector x_t into a $k \times 1$ vector $z_t = P'x_t$ with the following properties:

(a) The k elements of z_t are mutually orthogonal.

(b) The eigenvalues associated with the k respective z_t's equal the *variances* of the components of z_t.

The first principal component is the linear combination of the x_t's (with norm of the weights constrained to 1) with the most variance, while the second component is the linear combination (orthogonal to the first one) with the next highest variance, and so on.

Thus, in principal components analysis, we seek a z_t that satisfies

$$z_t = P'x_t,$$

where the components of z_t are mutually orthogonal, so that $Ez_t z_t' = D$ is a diagonal matrix; and where successive rows of P' are orthogonal and of unit norm, so that $P'P = I$. The eigenvector decomposition of the covariance matrix V of x_t delivers the appropriate linear transformation P of x_t.

The eigenvector p_1 that is associated with the largest eigenvalue of D is called the *first principal component* of x_t. This eigenvector solves the problem of maximizing over p_1 the second moment $E(p_1'x)^2 = p_1'Vp_1$, subject to the unit norm side condition $p_1'p_1 = 1$. The first-order necessary condition for this problem is

$$(V - dI)p_1 = 0,$$

where $d/2$ is the Lagrange multiplier on the constraint. Evidently, $E(p_1'x)^2 = p_1'Vp_1 = d^2||p_1||^2 = d^2$ is maximized by choosing d to be the largest eigenvalue of V and p_1 to be the associated eigenvector. The second principal component maximizes $E(p_2'x_t)^2$ subject to $p_2'p_2 = 1$ and $p_1'p_2 = 0$, and so on. Furthermore, d_i^2 is the second moment of $z_{it} = p_i'x_t$.

Data reduction

Sometimes principal components analysis is used for building linear models designed to summarize the most important source of (generalized) variance within a data set x_t. For example, in economic time series data, the first one or two principal components often account for a dominant proportion of variance. The first principal component is a linear combination of the data along which most of the variation occurs.[9]

Estimation

Estimation of principal components proceeds by substituting for Ex_tx_t' the sample moment matrix $T^{-1}\sum_{t=1}^{T} x_tx_t'$. To estimate principal components, one simply computes the eigenvalues and normalized eigenvectors of the sample moment matrix.[10]

Factor analysis

Factor analysis represents the covariance within a $k \times 1$ vector x_t of observables in terms of their mutual dependence on a smaller $\ell \times 1$ vector f_t of hidden 'factors,' where $\ell << k$. The second-moment matrix $V = Ex_tx_t'$ is restricted to be the sum of a matrix of rank ℓ and a diagonal matrix

$$V = LL' + D,$$

---

[9] That is, for such data, the covariance matrix is 'ill-conditioned'.

[10] The method of Oja (1982) for grouping data amounts to a recursive implementation of principal components analysis.

where L is a $(k \times \ell)$ matrix and D is a $(k \times k)$ diagonal matrix. The model can also be represented as

$$x_t = L f_t + \epsilon_t,$$

where $E f_t f_t{}' = I_\ell$, the $(\ell \times \ell)$ identity matrix, $E \epsilon_t \epsilon_t' = D$, and $E f_t \epsilon_t' = 0$. The $(\ell \times 1)$ vector f_t is composed of *hidden factors*, while the $(k \times 1)$ vector ϵ_t contains idiosyncratic noises.

The model asserts that all of the covariance within the x_t vector is intermediated via the action of a much smaller number of hidden factors. A classic use of the model is interpreting students' test scores. Here x_t is a vector of student t's scores on k tests on various subjects, such as history, French, English, algebra, physics, and so on. It is posited that there are two hidden orthogonal factors, 'mathematical intelligence' and 'verbal intelligence,' that explain the structure of correlations among the test scores. A second example comes from the field of business cycle analysis, where it is possible to read Burns and Mitchell (1946) as asserting that there is one underlying factor called 'business conditions' or the 'business cycle,' dependence upon which intermediates most or all of the correlation among measures of economic activity at business cycle frequencies.[11]

For a given sample $\{x_t\}_{t=1}^{T}$, let $S_T = \sum_{t=1}^{T} x_t x_t'/T$. For a Gaussian likelihood function, maximum likelihood estimation seeks values for L, V that satisfy the normal equations

$$V^{-1}(V - S_T) V^{-1} L = 0$$
$$\text{diag } V^{-1}(V - S_T) V^{-1} = 0.$$

See Jöreskog (1967) for efficient 'off-line' methods of solving these normal equations. In the spirit of stochastic approxima-

---

[11] See Sargent and Sims (1977) for remarks about the history of this interpretation of Burns and Mitchell (1946), and for details about how the static factor analysis model can be made dynamic via its application in the frequency domain in a way to encompass this interpretation of Burns and Mitchell.

tion, one might use the 'on-line' algorithm

$$L_{t+1} = L_t + (1/t)(V_t^{-1}(V_t - x_t x_t')V_t^{-1}L_t)$$
$$V_{t+1} = V_t + (1/t)\text{diag}(V_t^{-1}(V_t - x_t x_t')V_t^{-1})$$
$$D_t = V_t - L_t L_t'.$$

Overfitting and choice of parameterization

Economists are familiar with the phenomenon of *overfitting*. The term overfitting is meant to describe a circumstance in which a researcher can get a good fit for the data set in hand by estimating so many parameters that out of sample the model does much worse than an alternative model that fits fewer parameters, thereby giving up the ability to fit the sample data as well in exchange for increased precision of the estimated parameters.[12] Figures 1 and 2 show a standard example in which two 'wrong' models (polynomials in time) are fitted to a random walk (i.e., a y_t process $y_t = y_{t-1} + \epsilon_t$, where ϵ_t is a serially uncorrelated Gaussian variable). Evidently, the higher-order model fits much

---

[12] Statisticians have dealt with the problem of overfitting by adopting criteria for choosing among parameterizations that penalize models with more parameters. The Schwarz Information Criterion (Schwarz 1978) is one widely used criterion; others are described by Rissanen (1989). Chung-Ming Kuan and Tung Liu (1991) apply and discuss some of these criteria in selecting among univariate models that are designed to predict future exchange rates. They report the results of employing the 'Predictive Stochastic Complexity' criterion of Rissanen. This criterion works as follows. Given a function $h(x, \theta)$ designed to 'forecast' y, and given a sample of length T observations, compute the mean square of so-called *honest* prediction errors, namely,

$$(T - k)^{-1} \sum_{t=k+1}^{T} (y_t - h(x_t, \hat{\theta}_{t-1}))^2,$$

where $\hat{\theta}_{t-1}$ is estimated using data only through time $k - 1$. The model with the smallest value is the one selected by this criterion. Kuan and Liu find that it is difficult to pin down systematic nonlinearities that can be used to predict exchange rates better than by using a random walk theory of exchange rates.

better within the sample, but will do a much worse job of predicting y if it is extrapolated.

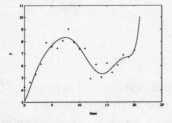

Figure 1.   An eight-order polynomial in time fitted to 21 observations on a random walk.

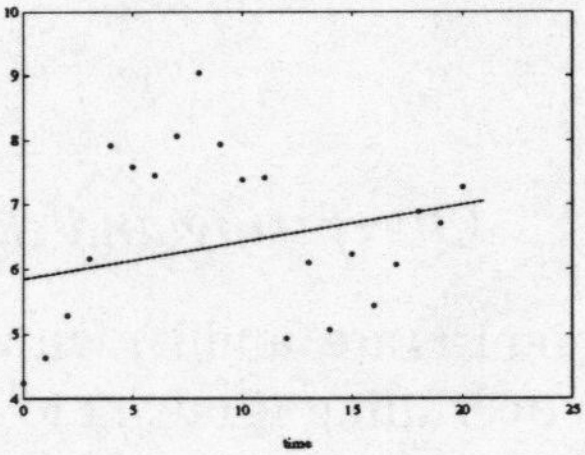

Figure 2.   A first-order polynomial in time fitted to 21 observations on a random walk.

Parameterizing vector autoregressions

The autoregressive representation has too many parameters to be useful for applications to the short data sets that economists work with. It imposes little more than that $C_z(k)$ are well defined, i.e. that the process is covariance stationary. In terms of describing a data-generating mechanism, the representation affords no economies in terms of numbers of parameters *vis à vis* either the entire list of covariance matrices $C_z(k)$ or, equivalently, the *spectral density* $S_z(\omega) = \sum_{-\infty}^{\infty} C_z(k) \exp(-i\omega j)$. (Even though it provides no economies in terms of representation, the vector autoregression might provide insights.)

Applying vector autoregressions requires adopting special versions in which the numbers of parameters are kept small relative to the length of the data sets being studied. Economists have devised differing specializations designed to render the vector autoregressive model applicable.

Rational expectations macroeconomists and econometricians have devised one set of procedures for reducing the number of parameters. In addition to restricting the lag-length (instead of fitting an infinite-order vector autoregression, they fit models in which z_t depends on only m lagged values of itself), they typically restrict the number of coefficients that describe the cross-variable dynamics. They use theories that imply a particular class of functions $A_j = A_j(\theta)$ expressing each coefficient matrix in the vector autoregression as a function of a much smaller number of free parameters θ.[13] These parameters are interpreted as describing the preferences, technologies, and information sets of the agents whose behavior is determining z_t. Such rational expectations models typically claim to be *complete* and *fully interpreted* models in the sense that they purport to describe the covariation through time of all of the variables modelled in ways consistent with general equilibrium theory, with the parameters being economically interpretable as preference, technology, or information parameters.

Sims, Litterman, and their co-workers have invented a different way of coping with the overfitting problem. In principle, their procedures do not restrict the number of parameters (beyond their use of some restrictions on lag lengths), but work by heavily exploiting some of the computational features associated with a recursive form of estimation that is applicable to vector autoregressions. Rather than adopting a function $A_j = A_j(\theta)$ as the rational expectations modellers do, Sims and Litterman carry along all of the elements of the A_j's as free parameters, but restrict the initial coefficients and covariance matrix. Then they update *all* of the coefficients via recursive least squares. Evidently, their estimation procedures (or sometimes important parts of them) have interpretations as stochastic approximation algorithms.[14] Litterman and Sims have devoted much effort to devising specifications of these initial conditions that are designed to forecast macroeconomic time series well out of the sample used to estimate the parameters. Litterman and

[13] Work along the lines of Hansen and Sargent (1980, 1981) and Kydland and Prescott (1982) fits within this category.

[14] Doan, Litterman, and Sims (1984) describe a set of procedures for *searching* over some parameters (or *hyperparameters*) that pin down the initial conditions of the least squares recursions.

Sims's choice of these initial conditions has involved less formal use of economic theory than that used by rational expectations econometricians in deducing their functions $A_j = A_j(\theta)$. [15]

Statistics for bounded rationality

The boundedly rational agents that we shall put into our example economic environments will all use versions of the stochastic approximation algorithm to estimate decision functions or parameters. This strategy for modelling boundedly rational agents starts from the observation that first-order conditions for stochastic estimation and optimization take exactly the form of the equation being solved by stochastic approximation, namely,

$$(4) \qquad\qquad EQ(z_t, \alpha) = 0.$$

Further, stochastic approximation is designed to solve this equation under the conditions of limited knowledge (i.e., insufficient knowledge to use the differential calculus or the expectational calculus) with which we want to endow our artificially intelligent agents.

---

[15] Sargent and Sims (1977) and Litterman and Sargent experimented with a factor analytic method for restricting the dimensionality of the parameter space for vector autoregressions. They used the frequency domain version of the factor analysis model, which assumes that the spectral density matrix of z_t can be written

$$S_z(\omega) = L(\omega)L(\omega)' + D(\omega),$$

where $L(\omega)L(\omega)'$ is a matrix of rank k for each ω, and $D(\omega)$ is a diagonal matrix. This is equivalent to assuming that z_t has the time domain representation

$$z_t = \sum_{j=-\infty}^{\infty} L_j f_{t-j} + u_t,$$

where u_t is an $(n \times 1)$ vector process, each component of which is orthogonal at all leads and lags to each component of the $(k \times 1)$ vector of hidden factors f_t. Sargent and Sims (1977) and Litterman, Quah, and Sargent (1984) used this model with $k = 1$ to represent and evaluate Burns and Mitchell's ideas about the business 'reference cycle.'

We shall see stochastic approximation algorithms applied over and over again, in superficially different contexts. Sometimes they will be used with versions of boundedly rational agents' first-order conditions that come from estimation problems like those described in this chapter. Stochastic approximation algorithms will also be used where (4) is interpreted as the 'Euler equation' from a boundedly rational agent's optimum problem.

Before handing stochastic approximation algorithms to our boundedly rational economic agents, we turn in the next chapter to survey some of the themes in the recent literature on neural networks and other forms of artificial intelligence. In reading this material, watch for stochastic approximation methods to make appearances.

4
Networks and Artificial Intelligence

This chapter describes some artificial devices that display 'intelligence.' Some of them memorize and recall patterns. Others represent and learn nonlinear decision rules. Most of the devices come from the recent 'connectionist' literature on neural networks. As Halbert White has taught, a student of econometrics will recognize many parallels between the connectionist literature and his own, in terms of problems and the methods. The connections between the literatures on neural networks and econometrics provide additional perspective on our characterization of bounded rationality as a program to populate models with devices that mimic econometricians.[1]

The perceptron

The simplest neural network is a single-layer perceptron, a model of the interaction of k input neurons $x_{it}, i = 1, \ldots, k$, with one output neuron y_t. The neurons are elements $x_i \in X$ and $y \in Y$, where the spaces X, Y can be specified in various ways. For example, for 'Ising neurons,' $X = \{-1, 1\}$; for classification perceptrons we take $Y = \{0, 1\}$. The perceptron model is

$$y_t = S\left(\sum_{i=1}^{k} w_i x_{it}\right)$$

or

$$y_t = S(w' x_t),$$

where w and x_t are each $(k \times 1)$ vectors, and S is a 'squasher'

---

[1] Useful references on some of the material in this chapter are Müller and Reinhardt (1990), Hertz, Krogh, and Palmer (1991), and Kosko (1992).

function, i.e. a monotonically nondecreasing function that maps **R** onto $[0, 1]$. Three popular squasher functions are:

1. The Heaviside step function:

$$S(z) = \begin{cases} 1, & \text{for } z \geq 0; \\ 0, & \text{for } z < 0. \end{cases}$$

2. The 'sigmoid function':

$$S(z) = \frac{1}{1 + e^{-z}}.$$

3. Any cumulative distribution function, e.g. the normal c.d.f.:

$$S(z) = \frac{1}{\sqrt{2\pi}\sigma} \int_{-\infty}^{z} \exp\left(\frac{-x^2}{2\sigma^2}\right) dx.$$

A perceptron is depicted graphically in Figure 1. Input x_{it} is weighted by w_i, inputs are summed across i, then the sum is squashed to yield output y_t. With the Heaviside squasher function, the neuron is either 'on' ($y_t = 1$) or 'off' ($y_t = 0$). For non-negative inputs, a positive weight w_i from input i to the neuron is called an 'exciting' connection, and a negative weight is called an 'inhibiting' connection, because such connections make it more or less likely that the neuron will 'fire.'

The perceptron as classifier

For a given set of weights w, a perceptron acts as a *classifier*. For example, let there be two classes of people, American football players ($y = 1$) and economists ($y = 0$). Let x_t be a vector of characteristics, say weight and salary, of individual t.[2] When we present the perceptron with x_t for economist t, we want the perceptron to eject output $y_t = 0$, and when we input the characteristics of a football player, we want the perceptron to

---

[2] Most American football players are heavier than the average person. Some economists are also heavier than the average person.

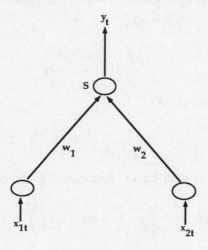

Figure 1. A perceptron. Values of two inputs x_{it} for $i = 1, 2$ are multiplied by w_i; the results are added together, then operated upon with the 'squasher' function S to produce the output y_t.

say $y_t = 1$. With the Heaviside step function as the squasher, the neuron 'fires' ($y_t = 1$) if and only if $w'x_t \geq 0$. With one of the other two squasher functions above, the value of y_t could be interpreted as the probability that an individual is a football player.

Perceptron training

Suppose that we have observations on k characteristics of two distinct predetermined populations, again say economists, whom we have labelled $y_t = 0$, and football players, whom we have labelled $y_t = 1$. We want to fit the perceptron to these data, which means that we want to estimate the weight vector w. We have a 'training sample' $\{y_t, x_t\}_{t=1}^T$, where t denotes a particular individual. The perceptron training problem is to choose w to minimize $\sum_{t=1}^T (y_t - S(w' x_t))^2$. This is a nonlinear least squares problem. The literature on perceptrons describes various algorithms of the iterative form

$$w_t = w_{t-1} + \gamma_t \nabla S(w_{t-1}, x_t)(y_t - S(w'_{t-1} x_t)),$$

where $\{\gamma_t\}$ is a nonincreasing sequence of positive numbers, and $\nabla S(w, x)$ is the gradient of S with respect to w. One scheme is to pick γ_t equal to a small positive constant, and repeatedly to run the sample $\{y_t, x_t\}_{t=1}^T$ through the algorithm until convergence occurs. Implementations of nonlinear least squares found in the econometrics literature also apply directly.

Perceptrons and discriminant analysis

There is evidently a close connection between a perceptron and a simple linear discriminant function. Early work on the perceptron focused on determining which classes of objects could and could not be separated by a perceptron, with negative early results by Minsky and Papert (1969) contributing to a long period of disenchantment. Minsky and Papert's negative judgement about the perceptron was based on its inability to represent a *nonlinear* discriminant function. Enthusiasm for perceptrons revived in the early 1980s when it was recognized that networks of perceptrons could approximate any nonlinear discriminant function.[3]

---

[3] In-Koo Cho (1992) shows that a pair of single-layer perceptrons can represent all subgame-perfect strategy pairs in an infinitely repeated (undiscounted) prisoners' dilemma game. A key part of his demonstration is that a single-layer perceptron is 'discriminating enough' for the situation each player confronts. Cho shrewdly exploits the ease with which a perceptron can implement a 'trigger strategy' via a squasher function. For another infinitely repeated two-player game, Cho shows that a single-layer perceptron is too simple (because it is unable to discriminate among situations adequately), but that a network with one hidden layer is able to encode all subgame-perfect equilibrium strategies.

Feedforward neural networks with hidden units

The perceptron is the building block out of which many types of neural networks are constructed. By arranging banks of perceptrons into rows and linking elements of successive rows via weighted summation operators, we construct a *feedforward neural network*. Halbert White and various co-workers[4] have shown that feedforward neural networks are best regarded as approximators of nonlinear functions g mapping vectors $x \in X$ into vectors $y \in Y$.

A feedforward neural network with one hidden layer is described by the two equations

(1)
$$y_t = \theta_0 + \sum_{j=1}^{q} \theta_j a_{tj}$$

$$a_{tj} = S\left(\sum_{i=1}^{k} w_{ji} x_{it}\right).$$

The second equation describes the output a_{tj} of hidden unit j, which is simply a perceptron. The first equation generates the output y_t of the network by taking an affine function of the $(q \times 1)$ vector a_t of outputs of the hidden units. The parameters of the network are the weights w_{ji} and θ_j. The network can be represented compactly as

(2)
$$y_t = \theta_0 + \sum_{j=1}^{q} \theta_j S(w_j{}' x_t).$$

An example of such a network is depicted in Figure 2.

The literature has addressed two issues about models of this class: the issue of *approximation* or *representation*, and the issue of *estimation*. The approximation literature describes the class of functions $g : X \to Y$ that can be arbitrarily well approximated by model (2). Hornik, Stinchcombe, and White (1989) have

---

[4] Including Ronald Gallant, Kurt Hornik, and Maxwell Stinchcombe.

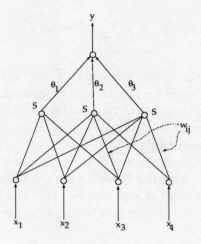

Figure 2. A feedforward neural network. The network takes inputs x_i, multiplies them with weights w_{ij} and adds over i to get the input into the hidden node j, operates on the input $\sum w_{ij} x_i$ into each hidden node j with the 'squasher' function S, then multiplies with θ_j and adds to get the output y.

shown that a very wide class of functions can be approximated by (2).[5] The parameter that controls the quality of approximation is q, the number of hidden units. For a given q, the best mean-square approximator to a function $g(x)$ is determined by

[5] They show that, if enough hidden units are included, then any Borel measurable function from one finite dimensional space to another can be approximated arbitrarily well. Barron (1991) showed that to achieve the same approximation rate a feedforward network uses only linearly many parameters ($O(qn)$), while polynomial, spline, and trigonometric expansions use parameters that grow exponentially ($O(q^n)$).

the values of (θ, w) that minimize the squared norm

(3) $$\| g(x) - \theta_0 + \sum_{j=1}^{q} \theta_j S(w_j{}'x) \|^2 .$$

Here $\| \cdot \|^2$ is the L_2 norm. For a given q, the best approximator can be found by variations on Newton's method. The approximation literature comforts us by assuring us that, if we select q large enough, we can find a (θ, w) that make this mean squared error as small as we might want.

The *estimation* problem occurs when we are given a sample $\{y_t, x_t\}_{t=1}^{T}$ and a particular model of the form (2), with fixed q, and want to estimate the parameters. This is a version of the nonlinear regression problem. The model to be estimated can be written in the form

$$y_t = g(x_t, \beta) + \epsilon_t,$$

where we have stacked the parameters (θ, w) into the vector β. Estimation can proceed by utilizing one of the algorithms based on equations (16) or (17) of the previous chapter. The 'training' algorithms discussed in the literature all use versions of these iterations. There exist examples of such 'on-line' algorithms that have asymptotic properties equivalent to 'off-line' algorithms. However, for small samples one can generally do better by using an 'off-line' algorithm.

Recurrent networks

The second equation of (1) can be modified in a way that lets us model dynamics. For example, we can specify

$$a_{tj} = S(w_j{}'x_t + \delta_j{}'a_{t-1}),$$

where a_{t-1} is the vector of values of $a_{t-1,j}$, and δ is a vector of additional parameters. This kind of network has been used by

Elman (1988) , and captures feedback to the hidden units from past values of hidden units. Alternatively, we could also specify

$$a_{tj} = S(w_j{}'x_t + \gamma_j{}'y_{t-1}),$$

where γ_j is a vector of parameters. In the special case that $w_j = 0$ for all j, this is an autonomous dynamic system, one that can be used to represent the systematic part of a nonlinear vector autoregression; this specification is a version of a *Hopfield network*, to which we now turn.

Associative memory

This section describes a class of networks that store memorized patterns and solve some signal extraction problems. The simplest version of such a network is a dynamic system that has locally stable rest points at a predetermined number of memorized patterns. The network is designed so that, when a corrupted version of one of these patterns is injected, the network quickly converges to the closest memorized pattern.[6]

Autoassociation

Suppose that patterns are represented as vectors of length N written in the binary alphabet $\{1, -1\}$, so that a particular pattern is expressed as a vector of 1's and -1's of length N. There are p patterns that we want memorized. Let these patterns be represented by the vectors $\sigma^1, \sigma^2, \ldots, \sigma^p$, which we arrange into the $(N \times p)$ matrix σ. We assume that the patterns are *orthogonal*, by which we mean that $\sigma'\sigma = N \cdot I_p$ where I_p is the $p \times p$ identity matrix. It is assumed that p is small relative to N. The p patterns correspond to 'Platonic ideals.'

---

[6] Hertz, Krogh, and Palmer (1991) and Müller and Reinhardt (1990) are good references on the material in this section. Müller and Reinhardt provide an example in which a Hopfield network is used to 'read' noise corrupted letters encoded in pixels via 'Ising neurons.'

When the system is presented with an error-ridden signal in the form of a vector s of length N with elements $\{-1, 1\}$, we want to know which pattern σ^p is the closest to the signal, as measured by the distance

(4) $$H_\mu(s) = \sum_{i=1}^{N} (\sigma_i^\mu - s_i)^2, \quad \mu = 1, 2, \ldots, p.$$

That is, we want to know the value of $\mu \in (1, 2, \ldots, p)$ for which the distance given by (4) is smallest. One procedure is simply to compute $H_\mu(s)$ for each value of μ, and then select the one yielding the lowest value of H_μ. For large values of p, this can be a time consuming process.

The idea of *associative memory systems* is to create a dynamic system

(5) $$s(t + 1) = f(s(t))$$

with the following two properties:

(a) Every memorized pattern is a fixed point of f:

(6) $$\sigma^k = f(\sigma^k), \quad k = 1, \ldots, p.$$

(b) Every σ^k is locally stable. That is, around each σ^k, there is a neighborhood $N(\sigma_k)$ such that, for $s_0 \in N(\sigma_k)$, iterations on f starting from s_0 converge to σ^k.

If such a dynamic system can be crafted, 'recalling from memory' is just the process of iterating on f starting from a presented pattern. We want the convergence to occur rapidly.

Figure 3 portrays a 'phase diagram' of a Hopfield network with four memorized patterns. The arrows in the diagram indicate how the network is locally stable about each of the memorized patterns.[7]

---

[7] A problem in constructing associative memory models is that sometimes

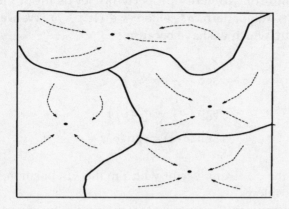

Figure 3. A Hopfield network. The network has four 'mem-orized patterns' that are attractors for the net's dynamics.

It is easy to create a mapping f with the desired properties. We use the *Hopfield network*

$$(7) \qquad\qquad s(t + 1) = \text{sgn}\,(w\,s(t)),$$

where w is an $N \times N$ matrix and sgn is the 'sign' function that maps real-valued vectors into vectors of binary numbers, mapping positive components into +1, negative components into -1. A common way to choose w is according to *Hebb's rule*:

$$(8) \qquad\qquad w = \frac{1}{N}\,\sigma\sigma'.$$

the builder inadvertently puts 'spurious patterns' into the network, so that the network recalls patterns that weren't taught to it. Notice that the construction in the text assures that the 'memorized patterns' are rest points of the network, but does not preclude the presence of other rest points.

It is straightforward to show that Hebb's rule builds in properties (a) and (b). To verify property (a), let us input into the
network the kth pattern, σ^k, where $k \in (1, \ldots, p)$. We want σ^k
to be output, which we have because

$$\sigma^k = \text{sgn}\left(\frac{1}{N}\, \sigma\sigma'\, \sigma_k\right)$$

$$= \text{sgn}\left(\sigma\left(\frac{1}{N}\, \sigma'\, \sigma_k\right)\right)$$

$$= \text{sgn}\,(\sigma e_k) = \text{sgn}\,(\sigma^k) = \sigma^k$$

Here e_k is the $p \times 1$ unit vector with 1 in the kth position, 0's in
all other positions.[8]

To study property (b), suppose that we input a noise-corrupted
version of pattern σ^k, s^k, where s^k agrees with σ^k except for
sign reversals at n randomly selected positions. We set the
dynamic system in motion starting from $s_0 = s^k$, and compute

$$s_1 = \text{sgn}\left(\frac{1}{N}\, \sigma\sigma'\, s^k\right)$$

$$= \text{sgn}\left(\frac{1}{N}\, \sigma(\sigma' s^k)\right)$$

$$= \text{sgn}\left(\sigma\frac{1}{N}
\begin{bmatrix}
r_1 \\
\vdots \\
r_{k-1} \\
N - 2n \\
r_{k+1} \\
\vdots \\
r_p
\end{bmatrix}
\right)$$

where $r_j = \sum_i \sigma_{ij}\, s_i^k$. The r_j terms can be expected to be
small because the pattern matrix σ is orthogonal, so long as the

---

[8] Notice that $\frac{1}{N}\,\sigma'\,\sigma_k = e_k$ because $\sigma'\sigma = NI_p$.

number of corrupted bits n is small. Thus we have

$$s_1 = \text{sgn} \left(\left(1 - \frac{2n}{N}\right) \sigma^k + \sum_{j \neq k} \frac{1}{N} \sigma^j r_j \right).$$

The terms $\sum_{j \neq k} \sigma^j r_j N^{-1}$ can be expected to have value on the order of $2\sqrt{n(p-1)/N}$, so that, as long as $p \ll N$ and $2n \ll N$, we have that

$$s_1 = \sigma^k,$$

indicating that convergence to the desired pattern occurs in one step.[9]

Correlated patterns

It is easy to modify Hebb's rule to accommodate correlated (but linearly independent) patterns. We now drop our earlier assumption that $\sigma'\sigma = N \cdot I_p$, and replace it by the assumption that

$$\sigma'\sigma = NV,$$

where V is a nonsingular matrix. We maintain system (7), but replace Hebb's rule (8) with the so-called 'projection rule':

$$w = \frac{1}{N} \sigma V^{-1} \sigma'.$$

It is easy to check that with this modified rule the rest points of $\text{sgn}[w\, s(t)]$ are $\sigma^1, \sigma^2, \ldots, \sigma^p$, as described, and that the system is locally stable about these rest points. To check the existence of σ^k as a fixed point, note that $w\sigma^k = \frac{1}{N} \sigma V^{-1}\sigma'\sigma^k = \sigma^k$.

---

[9] There is a literature on 'response times' in cognitive psychology in which subjects are asked to classify a specific example ('pelican') into one of a specified number of classes ('central banker,' 'bird,' 'congressperson'). Their times to respond are recorded and interpreted in terms of the closeness of the particular item to the ideal pattern. The Hopfield network is a useful device for interpreting these experiments.

Heterassociation

Hopfield networks can be 'wired' to remember sequences of patterns. Let $[\sigma^1, \sigma^2, \ldots, \sigma^p]$ represent a temporal ordering of patterns. When σ^k (or a corrupted version of it) is 'input' into the network, we want the 'output' from the network to be σ^{k+1}, where we understand that $\sigma^{p+1} = \sigma^1$, so that the memorized pattern is to be periodic. This is easily achieved by using a modified version of Hebb's rule. Let $\sigma = (\sigma^1, \ldots, \sigma^p)$, $\sigma'\sigma = NI_p$, $\sigma_+ = (\sigma^2, \sigma^3, \ldots, \sigma^p, \sigma^1)$. Let

$$ w = \frac{1}{N} \, \sigma_+ \, \sigma'. $$

Note that the system

$$ s(t+1) = \text{sgn}\,(w\,s(t)) $$

has the periodic solution $\sigma^{k+1} = \text{sgn}\,(w\sigma^k)$, for we have

$$ \text{sgn}\,(w\sigma^k) = \text{sgn}\,\left(\frac{1}{N} \, \sigma_+(\sigma' \, \sigma^k) \right) $$
$$ = \text{sgn}\,(\sigma_+ \, e_k) $$
$$ = \text{sgn}(\sigma^{k+1}) = \sigma^{k+1}, $$

where again e_k is the unit vector with one in the kth place.

Memorized patterns as energy minimizers

Associated with Hebb's rule (8) is the energy function [10]

$$ E(s) = -\frac{1}{2N} \, (s'\sigma\sigma' \, s). $$

By construction, the stored patterns σ^1, σ^2, $\ldots$, σ^p are each local minimizers of this function. In particular, note that

$$ E(\sigma^k) = -\frac{N}{2} $$

---

[10] If the formulas associated with Hebb's rule remind the economics student of things from econometrics, they should.

for σ^k, $k = 1, \ldots, p$, and that, since $s'\sigma^k \leq N$ for all s, we know that σ^k is a local minimizer. For the 'projection rule' $w = \frac{1}{N}\sigma V^{-1}\sigma'$, we have the associated energy function

$$E(s) = -\frac{1}{2N}(s'\sigma V^{-1}\sigma's).$$

Stochastic networks

Sometimes Hopfield networks are constructed that have spurious local rest points that the designer wants to avoid. When these rest points have small domains of attraction, they can be avoided by using a *stochastic network*. The idea is to modify the dynamics of the system by 'shaking' it at a rate that decreases over time. The purpose of shaking the system is to lower the probability that the system will come to rest at 'undesirable' local rest points and descend to better ones. Figure 4 contains an example of what is hoped for.[11] Introducing a random 'shaking' factor into Newton methods leads to what are called 'simulated annealing' methods.[12]

The dynamics of a network with neurons v_i, $i = 1, \ldots, N$, can be represented

$$(9) \qquad v_{i,t+1} = g\left(\sum_j w_{ij}v_{jt} - \theta_i\right),$$

where g is one of our 'squasher functions.' For example, we might use

$$g(x) = \tanh(x/T)$$

---

[11] Out of fear of getting stuck at an inferior local rest point, econometricians who estimate nonlinear models have the habit of trying a variety of starting values for their hill-climbing algorithms. Simulated annealing is inspired by the same fear, and amounts to a systematic way of choosing a set of starting values, and of perturbing directions and step sizes.

[12] This section relies heavily on Peterson and Söderberg (1992).

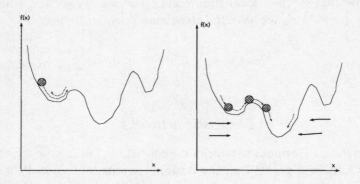

Figure 4a. Newton's method. Motion of a ball rolling down a hill under force of gravity. The ball may come to rest at a local minimum.

Figure 4b. A stochastic Newton method. Simulating annealing and 'stochastic network' methods 'shake' the system so that with probability arbitrarily close to one the ball will eventually escape being trapped in a local minimum.

as a squasher function for 'Ising neurons' that we want to constrain to take on values in $[-1, 1]$.[13] The variable $T \geq 0$ is a 'temperature' variable that governs the sharpness of the squasher function.

Combinatorial optimization problems

Neural nets have been used to solve constrained optimization problems that can be represented in the form: find a configuration of neurons $s_i \in \{-1, 1\}$, $i = 1, \ldots, N$, to minimize

$$C(s) = -(1/2) \sum_{i,j} w_{ij} s_i s_j + (\alpha/2) \left(\sum_i s_i \right)^2$$

[13] Or $g(x) = 0.5[1 + \tanh(x/T)]$, if we want the neurons to take values in $[0, 1]$.

or

(10) $$C(s) = -0.5s'ws + 0.5\alpha s's,$$

where w is a given matrix encoding costs, and α is a penalty-variable (or Lagrange multiplier). One approach to this problem would be to use the deterministic 'local dynamics,' i.e. those given by the Hopfield network,

(11) $$s(t + 1) = \text{sgn}((w - \alpha I)s(t)).$$

However, this algorithm typically fails to find a global minimum, and instead heads for the nearest local minimum.[14]

To get an algorithm with a better chance of descending to a global minimum, the deterministic local dynamics are sometimes replaced by stochastic ones. Let $\mu(s_i(t + 1) = \pm 1)$ be the probability that $s_i(t+1)$ is plus or minus 1. Then we can generate stochastic dynamics by setting

(12) $$\mu(s_i(t + 1) = \pm 1) = \frac{1}{1 + \exp(\mp 2(w_i's(t) - \alpha s(t))/T)}$$

where T is a non-negative temperature variable. This stochastic transition law produces a stochastic process with a stationary distribution over states given by the Boltzmann distribution

(13) $$\text{Prob}(s) = (1/Z)\exp(-C(s)/T),$$

where the normalization factor Z is

$$Z = \sum_s \exp(-C(s)/T).$$

As T approaches zero from above, this distribution concentrates more and more probability on the global minimum of the cost function (10).

---

[14] This local stability property is 'good' for models of associative memory, but 'bad' for schemes that iterate on first-order conditions from optimum problems.

The method of *simulated annealing* exploits this property. The algorithm works as follows. For a fixed initial $T = T_0 >> 0$ and a given initial configuration of neuron values s, use the stochastic dynamics, say via simulation methods, to compute a sample from the stationary distribution for that fixed T. This represents a sample drawn from the Boltzmann distribution (13). Now define an iterative process in which the system is 'annealed'; i.e., the temperature is gradually lowered, at a rate slow enough to permit the system approximately to settle into its stationary distribution at each temperature. In particular, lower the temperature, say according to $T_{k+1} = 0.9T_k$, where T_k is the temperature at the $(k+1)$th step; use the (approximate) stationary distribution from temperature T_k as an initial distribution; and use the transition dynamics at this new temperature to get an estimate of the probability distribution (13) associated with this new temperature. Continue in this way, lowering the temperature toward zero. Notice that as T approaches zero the probability given by (13) piles up near optimizing values of the state vector s.

This procedure is computational intensive, but has the virtue of assuring convergence to a global minimum of the cost function. The computational expense occurs at the step of computing the stationary distributions (13) at each temperature.

Mean field theory

The idea of mean field is to replace the stochastic dynamics with an associated *deterministic* dynamics that gives the correct direction of movement 'on average.'[15] The basic object of analysis is the *time average of neuron i at temperature T*, which we denote $< s_i >_T$ or $v_i =< s_i >$ for short. The variable $< s_i >= v_i$ is the average value of neuron i in the stationary equilibrium given

---

[15] See Brock (1992) for several applications of mean field dynamics to models of economics and finance.

by (13). The approximate *mean field* dynamics are given by

$$v_{i,t+1} = \tanh\left(-\frac{\partial C(v_t)}{\partial v_{it}}/T\right),$$

or

(14) $$v_{i,t+1} = \tanh\left(\sum_j (w_{ij} - \alpha)v_{jt}/T\right).$$

Equation (14) is a set of deterministic difference equations in the average states of the neurons. Notice the similarity between systems (9) and (14).

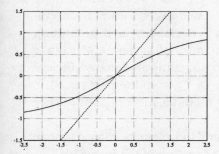

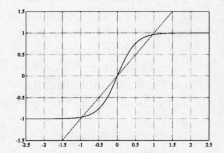

Figure 5a. The function $\tanh(x/T)$ with $T = 2$. Fixed points are at intersections with the dotted line of slope 1 through the origin.

Figure 5b. The function $\tanh(x/T)$ with $T = 0.5$. Fixed points are at intersections with the dotted line of slope 1 through the origin. At lower temperatures, the fixed point at 0 becomes unstable, and two stable fixed points near ± 1 appear.

The dynamics of the system (14) are known to exhibit behavior of two sorts, depending on the temperature T. At sufficiently high temperatures, the system moves to a steady state at $v_i^* = 0 \ \forall i$, which can be seen to be the fixed point of the tanh function (see Figures 5a and 5b). As the temperature is gradually lowered, a 'phase transition' is passed at a critical temperature

$T = T_c$, and the system moves to fixed points $v_i = \pm 1$ that approximate a solution of the minimization problem. Peterson and Söderberg describe methods for estimating the critical temperature T_c. These methods start from a Taylor series approximation of (14) around v_i^*, which yields the dynamics

$$\epsilon_{i,t+1} = (1/T) \sum_j (w_{ij} - \alpha)\epsilon_{jt},$$

where $v_i = v_i^* + \epsilon_i$. The stability of the local dynamics around $v_i^* = 0$ are determined by the eigenvalue of maximum modulus of the matrix

$$m_T = (w - \alpha I)/T.$$

For T large enough, the dynamics around v_i^* are evidently stable. However, for nontrivial w, there will exist a critical value T_c at which an eigenvalue of m_T will exceed unity in modulus, causing the linear dynamics to destabilize and prompting the nonlinear aspects of the dynamics of system (14) to take over. Peterson and Söderberg describe computationally efficient methods for estimating the value of T_c from the pair (w, α).[16] They also describe corresponding methods for similar but richer problems.

Here is Peterson and Söderberg's implementation of mean field dynamics to minimize a cost function of the form (10).

(a) Compute an estimate of the critical temperature T_c. Set $T_0 = T_c$, or $T_k = T_c$ for $k = 0$, where k is to index iterations.

(b) Initialize the (mean-field) neurons randomly to values $v_i \in [-1, 1]$.

(c) For $T = T_k$, iterate on the mean field dynamics (14).

---

[16] Peterson and Söderberg study both *synchronous* and *serial* implementations of the dynamics (14). The synchronous dynamics are simply (14). The serial or nonsynchronous dynamics are like the Gauss–Seidel algorithm: in updating a neuron i, the *latest* value of neuron j is used on the right side of (14).

(d) Reset temperature according to, e.g., $T_{k+1} = 0.9T_k$, and repeat step (c). Continue to iterate until the criterion function $C(s)$ 'settles down.'

Peterson and Söderberg (1992) provide several examples in which the mean field dynamics provide cheap and high-quality approximate solutions to some big optimization problems.

Shadows of things to come

Mean field theory uses a deterministic system whose dynamics approximate aspects of the average behavior of a random dynamical system. The deterministic system is formed by writing down the random dynamical system, then replacing random variables with their means at carefully chosen spots. This procedure has provided a cheap way of solving or approximately solving some high-dimension combinatorial optimization problems.

We shall encounter this kind of device again, in different contexts. In particular, we shall see how closely related arguments from the 'stochastic approximation' literature have been applied to study the convergence of systems of boundedly rational agents to rational expectations equilibria.

Local and global methods

Newton's method, which is the basis for many of the estimation methods that we have surveyed, has excellent local convergence properties, but can have difficulties globally. Simulated annealing and stochastic Newton methods are modifications designed to improve the global properties of Newton's method without eventually sacrificing its good local properties. We now turn to some global search algorithms proposed by Holland that depart more fundamentally from Newton's method.

The genetic algorithm

The genetic algorithm of John Holland was devised to find maxima of 'rugged landscapes' that lack the smoothness that Newton's method exploits.[17] Holland's idea was to turn loose on the landscape a population of sexually active artificial beings that would evolve itself to the top of the hill.

The genetic algorithm is a sequence of operations applied to a population of binary strings, which are strings of 0's and 1's of length S. Recall that each integer j in the collection $[1, 2, \ldots, \sum_{i=1}^{S} 2^{i-1}]$ can be represented as $j = \sum_{i=1}^{S} k_i 2^{i-1}$ where k_i is the value (0 or 1) in the ith position in the string. We can approximate a bounded set of real numbers $x \in X$ by setting $x = j/(b-a)$, where a, b, S are chosen to select the set that we want to approximate.

The algorithm begins with a collection of N binary strings of length S. We are given a non-negative function $f : X \to \mathbf{R}$, which we are to maximize. We encode values of $x \in X$, where X may be a vector space, in terms of binary bit strings. We are told how to compute $f(x)$ for any value of x within the domain defined by our encoding.

The algorithm uses the following operators.

1. *Evaluation of fitness.* For every value x_i for $i = 1, \ldots, N$, compute the value $f(x_i)$. Then compute the 'relative fitness' of x_i, defined to be $f(x_i)/\sum_{i=1}^{N} f(x_j)$.

2. *Fitness-proportional reproduction.* Make copies of the population by spinning a 'biased roulette wheel,' constructed by dividing a disk into N slices, with the probability of individual i's reproducing being set equal to its relative fitness $f(x_i)/\sum_{i=1}^{N} f(x_j)$. Spin the wheel N times, each time making a copy of the individual into whose slice the roulette ball comes to rest, thus making N copies. The copies constitute a new population of N individuals.

---

[17] Goldberg (1989) is a useful text on genetic algorithms.

3. *Mutation*. Independently subject each bit of each string to a small probability p_m of being flipped.

4. *Mating*. Randomly divide the population of N strings into $N/2$ equal subpopulations of 'males' and 'females.' Randomly match these subpopulations into $N/2$ pairs for the purpose of 'mating.' A pair (sometimes referred to in the literature as 'the happy couple') mates by drawing a random number that is uniformly distributed across the integers from 1 to $S - 1$. If the integer k is drawn, the male's and female's bit strings are each cut between the bit numbers k and $k + 1$, and two new strings are formed by joining the first k bits of the male string with the last $S - k$ bits of the female string, and *vice versa*. In this way are formed N 'children' strings. Extinguish the parents, and take the N children as the new population.

The algorithm starts by selecting a random sample of N strings, and then applying the four operators sequentially. After a new population is created via the mating operator, the algorithm applies the operator 1 again, continuing either for a prespecified number of rounds or else until a stable population of x's emerges. As the 'solution' of the original problem, select the fittest member x from the final population. The parameters of the algorithm are N, S, and the mutation rate p_m.

The reproduction operator increases the representation of relatively fit individuals in the population, but does nothing to find a *fitter* individual. The mutation and mating operators can add new elements to the population, while destroying old ones. If the mutation probability, p_m, is set too high, it slows or prevents convergence, and degrades the performance of the algorithm because it destroys fit individuals along with the unfit. But when the mutation rate is set to a very low value, mutation alone is a poor mechanism for injecting diversity into the population. The mating operator seems to be a very good device for probabilistically injecting diversity, while giving structures that have proved their fitness a shot at surviving.

This algorithm has proved its value in a variety of applications. It has some features of a *parallel* algorithm, both in the obvious sense that it simultaneously processes a sample distribution of elements, and in the subtler sense that, instead of processing individuals, it is really processing equivalence classes of individuals. These equivalence classes, which Holland calls *schemata*, are defined by the lengths of common segments of bit strings. The algorithm is evidently a random search algorithm, one that does not confine its searches locally. The mating operator, which lies at the heart of the algorithm, creates new strings, but only when it operates on a population within which there is already diversity. The beauty of this operator is that, while it creates new values of x (at the cost of destroying old ones), it does so in a way that preserves long sections of 'genetic structure,' i.e. segments of bit strings. Depending precisely on how a given problem has been encoded, this feature can embody a useful compromise between the principles of adventure and preservation.

The genetic algorithm is designed to produce a sequence of populations of organisms that moves up a fitness criterion f. The 'individuals,' i.e. the bit strings, do not 'learn'. (Each of them dies after one period.) Only the 'society' of the sequence of populations of bit strings can be regarded as learning. This feature makes it difficult to accept the genetic algorithm literally as a model of an individual 'brain.' It is much easier to relate to John Holland's *classifier system* as a model of an individual's brain or thought process.[18]

---

[18] Ellen McGrattan has applied genetic algorithms to estimate nonlinear rational expectations models. She first uses genetic algorithms to search for the vicinity of a maximum, then switches to a Newton method.

Classifier systems

The brain as a 'competitive economy'

John Holland conceived the 'classifier system' as an evolving collection of potential 'condition–action' statements that decide and learn. He used an alphabet for expressing the rules that permits more general statements to co-exist with less general statements. The statements compete with one another for the opportunity to decide. The classifier system incorporates elements of the genetic algorithm with other aspects in a way that represents a brain in terms that Holland describes as a competitive economy.

A classifier system consists of a more or less comprehensive list of 'if–then' statements called *classifiers* that map *conditions* into *actions*, and a set of rules for interpreting and altering these statements to make decisions through time. A classifier system has a list with a fixed number of classifiers. When a message from the environment enters the classifier system, in general, *several* of the classifiers will have their 'if' parts satisfied, but usually their 'then' parts will differ, in which case these classifiers are offering different advice ('Go on, say hello to her' versus 'Mind your own business'). Which classifier makes the decision is determined by an 'auction' among the relevant set of classifiers, with classifiers bidding with 'resources' accumulated via an accounting process that registers the consequences of past decisions. The accounting system is the vehicle by which the classifier system learns to alter its behavior over time.

More formally, a classifier system consists of the following objects.

1. *Bit strings (classifiers)*. A classifier is a bit string of fixed length, written over the trinary alphabet $0, 1, \#$, where $\#$ is interpreted as 'either 0 or 1' or 'I don't care.' The first part of each bit string is interpreted as encoding a 'condition' statement, while the remaining bits encode an 'action' statement. The presence of the $\#$ sign accommodates generalization.

2. *A decoding device.* When a state occurs in the environment, this device identifies which of a fixed collection of classifiers match in their 'condition' parts the condition prevailing in the environment. The device thereby identifies a set of classifiers, from which one is to be selected actually to make a decision at the moment.

3. *An accounting system.* A measure of value called *strength* is assigned to each classifier in the system at each point in time. Strengths for each classifier are updated over time in response to the utilities and costs that flow from the environment when the classifier acts. The accounting system computes cumulated averages of realized utilities net of costs. In sequential settings, the accounting system *taxes* classifiers operating at one stage, and awards the proceeds to the classifier at the immediately preceding stage of the decision tree whose decision moved the system to the position that gave the presently active classifier the opportunity to act. Setting up the accounting system in this way is important to induce decisions whose only rewards are that they facilitate subsequent decisions that will ultimately generate rewards.

4. *An auction system.* The auction system determines which of a set of matched classifiers is granted the right to act in any given situation. Two alternative auction principles are:
   (a) The highest strength rule gets to make the decision.
   (b) The right to make a decision is allocated probabilistically, with the probability of being granted the decision made equal to a rule's relative strength.

5. *A device for introducing new classifiers.* New classifiers are introduced in several situations.
   (a) *Uncovered situations.* The most obvious occurs when the environment produces a condition that matches no existing classifiers. In this situation, a new classifier is generated whose condition statement matches the existing environmental condition, and whose action part is randomly generated.

(b) *Try something new.* New classifiers are generated and old ones are occasionally extinguished in order to provide room for experimenting with untried actions.

(c) *Generalize and specialize.* New classifiers are synthesized to *generalize* (replace 0's and 1's with #'s), or to *specialize* (replace #'s with 0's or 1's in existing rules).

A two armed bandit

An example of Brian Arthur and Carl P. Simon illustrates a method for studying the limiting behavior of a classifier system in a very simple context. In particular, they showed how a classifier system would cope with a two armed bandit problem.[19] The ith arm pays a random variable x_{it} drawn independently and identically from a distribution F_i with mean μ_i. Assume that $\mu_1 > \mu_2$. A player must pull one arm for each t with $1 \leq t \leq T$, with his reward being his total payoffs. The player knows neither F_1 nor F_2.

Arthur let the classifier system consist of the two classifiers,

$$\# 0$$
$$\# 1.$$

Here the first entry encodes the 'condition' and the second entry encodes the 'action'; # means 'whatever the history of observations,' 1 means pull the first arm, and 0 means pull the second arm. The conditions of both classifiers are met all of the time. The first classifier plays arm 1 all of the time, and the second plays arm 2 all of the time. Let $\tau_i(t), i = 1, 2$, be a clock recording the cumulative number of times that arm i has been pulled as of time t, which equals the cumulative number of times that classifier i has acted. Arthur set up the accounting system

$$S_{i\tau_i} = S_{i\tau_i-1} + (1/\tau_i)(x_{i\tau_i} - S_{i\tau_i-1}),$$

[19] These results were presented by Arthur (1989b) and Simon in independent oral presentations at the Santa Fe Institute in March 1989.

where $S_{i\tau_i}$ is the 'strength' of classifier i after it has been rewarded with its payoff when its clock is at τ_i.

Arthur used a random device based on relative strengths to determine the advice of which classifier was followed at time t. In particular, at time $t + 1$, the system follows the advice of classifier 1 with probability π_{1t+1} given by

$$\pi_{1t+1} = S_{1\tau_1(t)}/(S_{1\tau_1(t)} + S_{2\tau_2(t)}).$$

By using methods of stochastic approximation, Arthur showed that the classifier system eventually 'probability-matches,' that is, plays the arms in fractions-over-time that are in proportion to their expected rewards.[20]

Design decisions

An author of a classifier system controls the list of states or conditions to encode, the scheme for encoding them, and the accounting system that distributes rewards and collects 'taxes.'[21] Thus, some 'hard wiring' goes into the construction of a classifier system, much of it being done with an eye to the particular problem at hand. In some environments, what is not hard-wired is the degree of generalization.

Generality versus discrimination

The problem of learning induces an incompletely understood tradeoff between 'general' rules (those with 'conditions' that are coarse and therefore are often met) and 'specific' rules (those with conditions that are fine and therefore less frequently met). An advantage of 'general' rules is that their conditions are frequently encountered, which means that their performance can be assessed frequently. A disadvantage is that they call for the

---

[20] See Arthur (1989b) for discussions of various ways of altering the classifier system to improve its performance.

[21] In sequential problems, the author must also link classifier sub-systems 'intertemporally' in a ways that permit learning to experience the rewards of patience. See Marimon, McGrattan, and Sargent (1990) for an example.

same action for all states that satisfy the condition. In effect, general classifiers give the advice: 'use a piece-wise constant decision rule over the subset of the state space that I cover.' Specific decision rules have the opposite advantages and disadvantages. They potentially permit fine-tuning the action to fit the specific point in the condition space, but they pay for that advantage by requiring longer histories of experience to learn.[22]

An interesting property of classifier systems is that they can be set up in ways that permit the degree of generalization or specificity to emerge adaptively. The presence of the # (or 'I don't care') symbol in the alphabet, together with devices designed either to generalize or specialize,[23] provide this capacity. The literature has some intriguing simulation examples in which different degrees of generalization have emerged in classifier systems, but at the present time little is known about general principles that determine their propensity to generalize.

Summary

In this chapter we have seen recursive least squares dynamics appear in many guises and contexts. There are evidently many fascinating connections between research lines being pursued within the 'connectionist' literatures that we have surveyed in this chapter and the econometrics and statistics literatures described in the preceding chapter. It is tempting (and would surely be worthwhile) to pursue those connections more broadly and deeply, but it is time for us to redirect our attention to our main task of discussing *economic* models of bounded rationality. In the next chapter we hand over some recursive least squares algorithms to artificial agents living within one of several particular economic environments, and watch what happens.

---

[22] This might remind the reader of tradeoffs between parametric and non-parametric estimation strategies in econometrics.
[23] See Marimon, McGrattan, and Sargent (1990).

5
Adaptation in Artificial Economies

This chapter puts adaptive agents into five different environments that have been analyzed in the rational expectations literature, thereby illustrating some of the different structures and possibilities in economic systems composed of such agents.

The first model, due to Bray, nicely illustrates many features of 'least squares learning' in a 'self-referential' system, including the temporary irrationality of adaptive forecasting rules and the possibility of their eventual rationality. The second model, a version of Samuelson's overlapping-generations model of money, illustrates how successive generations can adaptively climb their way to more or less complicated rational expectations equilibria, and how the rate of convergence can depend on details of the adaptation algorithm and the intricacy of what must be learned. The third example puts overlapping generations of adaptive agents into an environment with too many equilibria, namely, a multiple currency setting in which the substitution of adaptive for 'rational' agents is enough to render the exchange rate determinate, but history dependent. The fourth example is a version of the 'no-trade' environment of Jean Tirole, in which the 'problem' with the rational expectations equilibrium is its incredible efficiency in eliminating opportunities for trade based on disparate information; I show how replacing rational agents with adapting ones can serve temporarily to restore opportunities for trade and thereby create trading volume. The last example, Marcet and Sargent's model of investment under uncertainty with learning, is designed to illustrate how much 'coaxing' must be done by us and how much 'theorizing' must be done by our artificial agents for them to learn when their planning horizon is infinite.

The presentation in this chapter is informal. We spend most of our effort describing and simulating models. The chapter is concluded with a brief description of how the machinery of stochastic approximation can be used to attain analytical results about the limiting behavior of such models.

A model of Bray

Margaret Bray (1982) studied a model that exhibits several features of systems that are adapting their way to a rational expectations equilibrium. These features include:

(a) People use a forecasting scheme that would be optimal if the environment were stationary. But their learning causes the environment to be non-stationary, and their learning scheme suboptimal.

(b) Sometimes the system converges to a rational expectations equilibrium.

(c) If the system does not converge to a rational expectations equilibrium, it does not converge.

(d) The dimension of the 'state' of the system with learning is larger than the corresponding rational expectations equilibrium, because measures of people's beliefs are needed to describe the position and motion of the system.

In Bray's model, the environment would be stationary if people were to know the distribution of prices. The dynamics in the model all come from the adjustment of people's expectations, which vanish if and when people learn the equilibrium distribution of prices.

Bray assumed a 'cobweb'-like structure in which the equilibrium price p_t for a single commodity is determined by a market-clearing condition of the form

$$(1) \qquad\qquad p_t = a + bp_{t+1}^e + u_t,$$

where p_{t+1}^e is the price that market participants expect to prevail at time $t + 1$, and $\{u_t\}$ is an independently and identically distributed sequence of random variables with mean zero. To compute a rational expectations equilibrium, we note the absence of dynamics in either the structural equation (1) or the shock u_t, and so we *guess* that $p_{t+1}^e = \beta \; \forall t$, a constant that is independent of time. Substituting this guess into (1) gives $p_t = a + b\beta + u_t$, which implies $E_{t-1}p_t = a + b\beta$. Evidently, the guess is true if $\beta = a/(1 - b)$. Substituting this value of $\beta = p_{t+1}^e$ back into (1) shows that in a rational expectations equilibrium $p_t = \beta + u_t$.

In backing off rational expectations, Bray assumed that people form the expectation p_{t+1}^e by taking an average of past prices. For convenience, we use the notation $\beta_t = p_{t+1}^e$. In terms of a stochastic approximation algorithm, Bray's assumption about expectations can be represented as

$$(2) \qquad\qquad \beta_t = \beta_{t-1} + (1/t)(p_{t-1} - \beta_{t-1}).$$

Notice how this scheme uses only observations on prices through period $t - 1$ to form price expectations at time t.

Rewrite equation (1) by substituting β_t for p_{t+1}^e to get

$$(3) \qquad\qquad p_t = a + b\beta_t + u_t.$$

Given an initial condition for β, equations (2),(3) determine the evolution of (p_t, β_t) through time, where β_t is interpreted as people's expectation of what p_{t+1} will be.[1] Bray studied

---

[1] This model has the special feature that, in the rational expectations equilibrium, the unconditional expectation equals the conditional expectation, a consequence of there being no time-varying state variables in the rational expectations equilibrium.

the circumstances under which β_t and the distribution of p_{t+1}, which evolve interdependently, would converge to a rational expectations equilibrium. That is, she studied the conditions under which β_t would converge to the value $\beta = a/(1 - b)$.

For describing people's learning behavior, we can use a state vector $z_t = [p_t\ 1]'$, whose law of motion is evidently

$$(4) \qquad \begin{bmatrix} p_t \\ 1 \end{bmatrix} = \begin{bmatrix} 0 & a + b\beta_t \\ 0 & 1 \end{bmatrix} \begin{bmatrix} p_{t-1} \\ 1 \end{bmatrix} + \begin{bmatrix} 1 \\ 0 \end{bmatrix} u_t.$$

This system indicates that, when at time t people estimate the price next period to be β_t, they act to make the *best* prediction of next period's price be $a + b\beta_t$. Notice that in forecasting this way people are acting as if they believe (incorrectly) that the law of motion of the state is not (4) but rather

$$(5) \qquad \begin{bmatrix} p_t \\ 1 \end{bmatrix} = \begin{bmatrix} 0 & \beta \\ 0 & 1 \end{bmatrix} \begin{bmatrix} p_{t-1} \\ 1 \end{bmatrix} + \begin{bmatrix} 1 \\ 0 \end{bmatrix} v_t,$$

for some serially uncorrelated random process $\{v_t\}$ with mean zero, where β is a *constant*. When people perceive that the law of motion for z_t is governed by (5), their forecasting causes the actual law of motion to be (4).

Margaret Bray showed that, if $b < 1$, system (2),(3) will converge to a rational expectations equilibrium with probability one. She also noted that $b < 1$ is a necessary condition for convergence to a rational expectations equilibrium.[2] Furthermore,

---

[2] Marcet and Sargent (1989a) show that the limiting behavior of β is governed by the associated differential equation

$$(d/dt)\,\beta = a + (b - 1)\beta,$$

which is stable for $b < 1$. The right hand side of this differential equation can be expressed as $T(\beta) - \beta$, where $T(\beta)$ is the mapping from the *perceived* forecast of prices β to the *optimal* forecast of prices $a + b\beta$. Stephen DeCanio (1979) and George Evans (1985, 1989) used the operator $T(\beta)$ to define a notion of expectational stability. Marcet and Sargent (1989a) described a sense in which the operator $T(\beta) - \beta$ governs the convergence of least squares learning schemes in a class of models.

she showed that, if the system does not converge to a rational expectations equilibrium, it does not converge at all.[3]

Irrationality of expectations

Although the model's exogenous 'fundamentals,' i.e. the $\{u_t\}$ process and the parameters a, b, are stationary, the stochastic process for the price $\{p_t\}$ is nonstationary, because it is a piece of the joint process $\{p_t, \beta_t\}$ determined by (2),(3). This means that the expectations formation scheme (2), which is a sensible way to estimate a mean for a stationary process (e.g., for someone already living within the rational expectations equilibrium of this market), is suboptimal so long as expectations are being revised. The fact that β in (3) is moving through time, as described by the law of motion (4), means that β_t is itself a 'hidden state variable,' and that the system (4) should be augmented to include it. Substituting (2) into (3) and rearranging gives the following system:

$$(6) \quad \begin{bmatrix} p_t \\ 1 \\ \beta_t \end{bmatrix} = \begin{bmatrix} b/t & a & b(t-1)/t \\ 0 & 1 & 0 \\ 1/t & 0 & (t-1)/t \end{bmatrix} \begin{bmatrix} p_{t-1} \\ 1 \\ \beta_{t-1} \end{bmatrix} + \begin{bmatrix} 1 \\ 0 \\ 0 \end{bmatrix} u_t.$$

This is a nonlinear stochastic difference equation, which can be used to forecast prices with smaller mean squared error than given by the forecast β_t used by the people in the model. In particular, the expectation of p_t conditioned on the entire state $z_t^* = [\, p_{t-1} \quad 1 \quad \beta_{t-1} \,]'$ is equal to

$$(7) \quad Ep_t | z_t^* = a + (b/t)p_{t-1} + (b(t-1)/t)\beta_{t-1}.$$

Equation (7) gives the 'rational expectation' of price conditional on the full state vector $[p_{t-1} \ 1 \ \beta_{t-1}]$. This is the price that

---

[3] Jasmina Arifovic (1991) has studied a version of Bray's model in which Bray's representative least squares learner is replaced by a population of heterogeneous agents with heterogeneous beliefs. She applied a genetic algorithm to this environment, and found that the population can sometimes learn its way to a rational expectations equilibrium even when Bray's necessary condition $b < 1$ is violated.

would be forecast by an outside observer who knew that the price was determined by (2), (3), and who could observe (or compute) β_{t-1} as well as p_{t-1}. The failure of this conditional expectation to equal β_{t-1}, except after convergence, indicates the irrationality of the learning scheme.

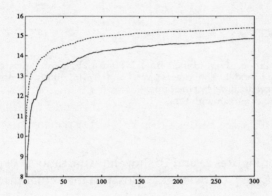

Figure 1. Simulation of $p_{t+1}^e = \beta_t$ (solid line) and the rational expectation $Ep_{t+1}|z_{t+1}^*$ (dotted line) in Bray's model starting from $\beta_0 = 8$. The variance of u_t was set at one. The conditional expectation $Ep_{t+1}|z_{t+1}^*$ is the best forecast of price that could be made by an outside observer who understood that agents are learning via Bray's scheme.

Figures 1 and 2 display aspects of a simulation of Bray's model in which we set $a = 5, b = 0.7, Eu_t^2 = 1$. The random process $\{u_t\}$ was generated with a Gaussian pseudo-random number generator. The rational expectations price is $a/(1 - b) = 16.667$. We started the system at $\beta_0 = 8$, an expected price far below the rational expectations price. Figure 1 shows the gap between the least squares forecast β_t and the conditional expectation $Ep_{t+1}|z_{t+1}^*$, which is large at first, then gradually diminishes

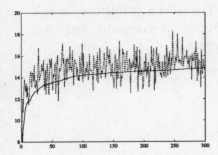 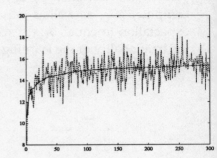

Figure 2a. Simulation of p_t (dotted line) and β_{t-1} in Bray's model. The forecast β_t on average underpredicts p_t, but the underprediction tends to diminish with time.

Figure 2b. Simulation of p_t (dotted line and $Ep_t|z_t^*$ in Bray's model.

over time. Figures 2a and 2b show how the rational expectations forecast $Ep_t|z_t^*$ on average is closer to the actual price p_t than is β_{t-1}.

Why not repair the irrationality indicated by the discrepancy between β_{t-1} and $Ep_t|z_t^*$ by going back to the original model and replacing β_{t-1} by $Ep_t|z_t^*$? Evidently, using this new theory of price expectations would require us to modify the actual law of motion for prices, which would render our new scheme suboptimal again. But we can use this new actual law of motion as our theory of expectations. This line starts us on a recursion, which has been taken up by Bray and Kreps (1987), who show that in the limit it leads us back to a rational expectations in which agents are learning 'within' the equilibrium, but not 'about' the equilibrium. Bray and Kreps argue against following this recursion to its limit if it is 'bounded rationality' that we are after. [4]

[4] See Mark Feldman (1987) for a study of the convergence of a model with a collection of Bayesian agents who start out with divergent priors. Also, see

Heterogeneity of expectations and size of the state

Bray's model assumes that all market participants have the same beliefs β_t. If we permit heterogeneity of beliefs, the effect is to add to the dimension of the true state in the appropriate counterpart to (6). For example, suppose that there are two classes of agents, differentiated only by the initial β_0, say β_0^a and β_0^b, which they use in a version of scheme (2), and that each of the two classes accounts for half of the market. Then the counterpart to (6) would include (β^a, β^b) as state variables. In this version of Bray's model, heterogeneity of beliefs would vanish as the system converges to a rational expectations equilibrium.[5]

An economy with Markov deficits

The second example is the overlapping-generations model of a monetary economy introduced by Paul Samuelson, and used extensively by John Bryant, Neil Wallace, and others to study issues of inflationary finance. We use this model to illustrate how:

(a) Learning can be modelled by having overlapping generations of agents adjust their behaviors relative to those of their ancestors in a utility increasing direction.

(b) The object about which agents are learning can be specified 'non-parametrically,' provided that agents are patient enough or lucky enough to be willing to learn how to behave on a state-by-state basis.

(c) Where the state is of high dimension, agents can be modelled as learning by using parametric decision rules.

(d) There is a close connection between algorithms to compute (approximate) equilibria and models of learning.

El-Gamal and Sundaram (1993).

[5] Marcet and Sargent (1989b) describe systems with heterogeneous beliefs in which heterogeneity remains in the rational expectations equilibrium because people are assumed to be differentially informed.

The economy consists of overlapping generations of two-period lived agents. At each date $t \geq 1$, there are born N identical agents who are endowed with w_1 units of a single consumption good when young, and w_2 units when old. Each young agent's preferences over a lifetime consumption profile (c_1, c_2) are ordered by the expected value of $u(c_1) + u(c_2)$, where $u(c) = \frac{c^{1-\delta}}{1-\delta}$, where $\delta > 0$.

There is a government that prints currency to finance government expenditures that are governed by a Markov chain

$$\pi(i, j) = \text{Prob}\{G_{t+1} = \bar{G}_j \mid G_t = \bar{G}_i\}.$$

We let $\bar{G} = [\bar{G}_1, \bar{G}_2, \ldots, \bar{G}_n]$ be the possible levels of government expenditures. The government's budget constraint is

$$G_t = (H_t - H_{t-1})/p_t,$$

where H_t is the stock of currency carried over by the young at t to $t + 1$, and p_t is the time t price level.

Stationary rational expectations equilibrium

The rate of return on currency between t and $t+1$ is $p_t/p_{t+1} = R_t$. We shall seek a *stationary* equilibrium in which the rate of return on currency is given by

$$R(i, j) = \text{rate of return on currency from } t \text{ to } t + 1$$
$$\text{when } G_t = \bar{G}_i \text{ and } G_{t+1} = \bar{G}_j.$$

Finding a stationary equilibrium requires solving a set of nonlinear equations in a set of vectors characterizing individual agents' optimal decisions. To derive these equations, we just write down everyone's first-order conditions and add market-clearing conditions. In a stationary equilibrium, savings are determined by an $(n \times 1)$ vector of state-dependent saving rates

where $s = [s_1, \ldots, s_n]$ and s_i is the saving rate when $G_t = \bar{G}_i$.[6]
A young agent's utility is given by

$$V(s_i) = u(w_1 - s_i) + \sum_j u(w_2 + s_i R(i,j))\, \pi(i,j),$$

for $i = 1, \ldots, n$ where u is an increasing and concave utility function. The first-order conditions with respect to s_i are
$V'(s_i) = 0 \; \forall i$ or

$$(8) \qquad u'(w_1 - s_i) = \sum_{j=1}^n u'(w_2 + s_i R(i,j)) R(i,j)\, \pi(i,j).$$

In a stationary equilibrium, the government's budget constraint,
namely, $\frac{H_t}{p_t} - \frac{H_{t-1}}{p_{t-1}} \frac{p_{t-1}}{p_t} = G_t$, can be written as

$$(9) \qquad h_j - h_i R(i,j) = \bar{G}_j$$

where $h_i = H_t/p_t$ when $G_t = \bar{G}_i$.

Finally, the condition that the supply of currency must equal
the demand can be written

$$H_t/p_t = s_t N$$

or

$$(10) \qquad h_i = s_i N.$$

---

[6] Models of this class typically have equilibria outside the class of stationary
'fundamental' equilibria that we are focusing on. In addition to a class of non-
stationary equilibria that David Gale (1973) studied, Azariadis, Guesnerie, Cass
and Shell have studied sunspot equilibria for such models. Michael Woodford
(1990) and George Evans (1989) have studied how collections of agents using
least squares learning schemes can converge to a sunspot equilibrium. To study
this question, Evans used a distinction between 'strong' and 'weak' expectational
stability, which focuses on whether or not convergence is robust to failure to
specify the *order* of the perceived autoregressive moving average process in a
way that is overparameterized with respect to an equilibrium process. 'Strong
stability' is the property that convergence to a rational expectations equilbrium
occurs when agents overparameterize the law of motion they are learning about.

To determine a stationary equilibrium, we have to solve equations (8), (9), and (10) for $(n \times 1)$ vectors s and h and an $(n \times n)$ matrix R of rates of return, where the s_i's satisfy $s_i \in (\frac{\bar{G}_i}{N}, w_1)$ and the elements of $R(i, j)$ are all positive. Notice that (9) and (10) imply

$$(11) \qquad R(i,j) = \frac{s_j N - \bar{G}_j}{s_i N}.$$

Substituting (11) into (8) gives the following set of n nonlinear equations to be solved for $[s_1, \ldots, s_n]$:

$$(12) \quad u'(w_1 - s_i) = \sum_{j=1}^{n} u'\left(w_2 + \frac{s_j N - \bar{G}_j}{N}\right) \cdot \frac{s_j N - \bar{G}_j}{s_i N} \, \pi(i, j)$$

Evidently, a stationary equilibrium exists if and only if (12) can be solved for $s = [s_1, \ldots, s_n]$ with $s_i \in (\frac{\bar{G}_i}{N}, w_1)$ for all i.

In general, the system of nonlinear equations (12) that determines a vector of *stationary* equilibrium saving rates s has multiple solutions. In addition to multiple stationary equilibria, there are nonstationary equilibria of the model, with a form resembling the 'bubble equilibria' of the models of money described in Chapter 2 and which we shall meet again in Chapter 6. Overlapping-generations models of the type we are using also have stationary 'sunspot equilibria,' that is, equilibria in which random variables (called 'sunspots' or 'extrinsic random variables') influence equilibrium prices and quantities only because they are expected to influence them.[7] The stability of sunspot equilibria under adaptive learning has been studied by Woodford (1990), Evans (1989), and Evans and Honkapohja (1992a).

---

[7] See Cass and Shell (1983), Azariadis (1981), and Azariadis and Guesnerie (1986).

A learning version

We use this environment as a setting in which successive generations of agents are 'learning' or 'evolving.' We want to watch how collections of adapting agents cope with the environment, and see whether and when they might eventually learn the rational expectations equilibrium. We can also watch how agents' learning varies as we alter the complexity of what they learn about, which in this setting is controlled by the number of states and the stochastic structure of the Markov process for government expenditures.

We endow agents with knowledge about their own utility functions, about the previous experiences of agents like themselves, and about the behavior of past and present government expenditures and prices. However, we do not give agents knowledge of the distributions of government expenditures, prices, and rates of return. Instead of knowing these distributions, agents must somehow use their historical observations, which might be arranged in the form of histograms or empirical probability distributions, to make decisions by some principle other than that of 'expected utility maximization with knowledge of equilibrium probability distributions.'

The economy with learning is identical with the model with rational agents, except that now the households consist of two classes (subsequences) of (adaptive) agents. We include two classes, called 'odd' and 'even,' because, in order to evaluate a person's saving decision, we wait until two periods' worth of consumption data for that person have become known. Odd agents reset a saving rate when t is odd, while even agents reset a saving rate when t is even. Odd agents learn from the past experiences of other odd agents, and even agents from the past experiences of other even agents. Agents of each class will be assumed to update their saving decisions based on the utility experienced by previous people of their type. In particular, they will adapt the decisions of their predecessors using a recursive

Newton–Raphson (or stochastic approximation) procedure.[8]

The *ex post* realized utility of a person who observed $G_t = \bar{G}_i$ and set $s_t = s_i$ when young at time t is

$$U(s_i) = u(w_1 - s_i) + u(w_2 + s_i \cdot R_t),$$

where R_t is the realized gross rate of return. The derivatives of realized utility with respect to the saving decision s_i are

$$U'(s_i) = -u'(w_1 - s_i) + u'(w_2 + s_i R_t) \cdot R_t$$
$$U''(s_i) = u''(w_1 - s_i) + u''(w_2 + s_i R_t) R_t^2.$$

Notice that, in a rational expectations equilibrium, $V'(s_{it}) = E_t U'(s_{it}), V''(s_{it}) = E_t U''(s_{it})$, where $E_t(\cdot)$ is the expectation conditional on $G_t = \bar{G}_i$. We want a learning algorithm to apply where people don't know these conditional expectations.

We assume that people use a Robbins–Monro algorithm, state by state. To set up the Robbins–Monro algorithm, we have to keep track of the number of periods an individual has been in a given state (i.e., observed $G_t = \bar{G}_i$) for each state. We let $t_j = 1, 2, \ldots$ for $j = o, e$ index the cumulative number of odd and even generations, respectively. For each state $i = 1, 2, \ldots, n$, we let $\tau_i^j(t_j)$, $j = o, e$, index the cumulative number of times that G_t has equalled $\bar{G}_i$. That is,

$$\tau_i^j(t_j + 1) = \begin{cases} \tau_i^j(t_j) + 1 & \text{if } G_{t_j} = \bar{G}_i \\ \tau_i^j(t_j) & \text{otherwise.} \end{cases}$$

We define the decreasing gain sequence $\gamma_\tau = 1/\tau$. The learning algorithm is then

---

[8] In models with agents who have an infinite horizon, it will obviously not work to let agents see and base adaptation of decisions on realizations of the infinite-horizon utility functional. Adaptation in settings with infinite-horizon agents has been modelled by endowing agents with versions of 'adaptive control' algorithms in which adaptation is confined to learning about a rule for forecasting state variables that are not controllable by the agent. The agent simply resolves a dynamic programming problem at each point in time with a revised forecasting rule. See Marcet and Sargent (1989a, 1989b) for some examples of such setups.

$$s^j(i, \tau_i^j + 1) = s^j(i, \tau_i^j) - \gamma_{\tau_i^j} M^j(i, \tau_i^j + 1)^{-1} U'(s^j(i, \tau_i^j))$$

$$M^j(i, \tau_i^j + 1) = M^j(i, \tau_i^j) + \gamma_{\tau_i^j} \left(U''(s^j(i, \tau_i^j)) - M^j(i, \tau_i^j) \right)$$

This algorithm is set up to promote the possibility that, as $\tau_i^j \to \infty$, we will have $M^j(i, \tau_i^j) \to E_t U''(s_i)$ and $s^j(i, \tau_i^j)$ will solve the first-order conditions $E_t U'(s_i) = 0$.

We assume the one-period utility function $u(c) = \frac{c^{1-\delta}}{1-\delta}$. In the experiments reported below, we assume the logarithmic specification $\delta = 1$.

We assume that young agents observe G_t before they make their saving decision. Agents of each type begin each period with an $(n \times 1)$ vector of saving rates $s^j(i, \tau_i), j = o, e$, 'learned' from ancestors of their own type, which they use as a state-contingent saving rule. When $G_t = \bar{G}_i$, the young at date t set savings according to $s_t = s^j(i, \tau_i^j)$.

The price level at time t is determined by the two equations

$$H_t = H_{t-1} + p_t G_t$$

$$H_t/p_t = s_t \cdot N,$$

which imply

$$p_t = H_{t-1}/(N s_t - G_t).$$

We require an initial condition H_0 for H_{t-1} at $t = 1$, and initial conditions for (M^j, s^j) for each of our two classes of agents.

We assume, as in the rational expectations version of the model, that G_t is a Markov chain with transition matrix π, where $\pi(i, j) = \text{Prob}\{G_{t+1} = \bar{G}_j \mid G_t = \bar{G}_i\}$.

Some experiments

Figures 3 and 4 report the results of using our learning algorithm. For each experiment, we set $\gamma_\tau = 1/\tau \; \forall \tau$, and we set inital conditions for $M_\tau = -I$.[9] We studied two economies,

---

[9] The initial conditions for the saving rates can be read from the graphs.

identical in all respects except for the stochastic process for government expenditures. In each economy, government expenditures follow a two-state Markov process with transition matrix π. In each economy, $w_1 = 20, w_2 = 10$ for each type of agent. In the first economy, government expenditures are identically zero in both states and $\pi_{ij} = 0.5 \; \forall \; (i,j)$. This implies that the rational expectations savings rates are 5 for each 'state' of government expenditures, and that the equilibrium rate of return on currency is unity always. In the second economy, government expenditures follow a Markov process with

$$\pi = \begin{pmatrix} 0.75 & 0.25 \\ 0.5 & 0.5 \end{pmatrix},$$

where the two states are $[\bar{G}_1 \; \bar{G}_2] = [0.8 \; 0]$. For the second economy, the equilibrium savings rates are $[4.211 \; 4.364]$, and the equilibrium rates of return are

$$R = \begin{pmatrix} 0.81 & 1.0362 \\ 0.7817 & 1.00 \end{pmatrix}.$$

For comparability, we model each of the economies as being driven by a two-state Markov process for government expenditures, though in the first economy this means that the agents are wastefully overfitting their saving function.

Figures 3 and 4 indicate that both economies are converging to the rational expectations savings rate. The convergence occurs more and more smoothly as time passes, a feature caused by the action of the γ_τ sequence.

In the zero expenditure economy, nothing stochastic is occurring. For this economy, convergence can be accelerated by using a *constant-gain* algorithm. This algorithm is formed by replacing the γ_τ by a constant. Besides accelerating convergence in constant environments, a potential advantage of constant-gain learning schemes is that they retain their flexibility to respond with the passage of time. A concommitant disadvantage is that

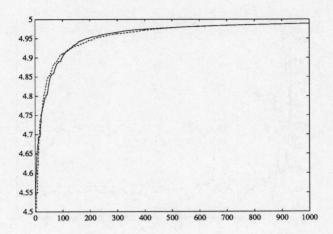

Figure 3. Simulation of savings rates of odd agents for stochastic approximation algorithm when $w_1 = 20, w_2 = 10, G_t = 0 \ \forall t$. The rational expectations equilibrium savings rates are 5 in each state. The saving rates (dark line for state 1, dotted line for state 2) are converging to the rational expectations saving rates.

their readiness to respond to recent occurrences prevents convergence to a rational expectations equilibrium when there are intrinsic shocks in the system. When intrinsic shocks are present, the most that can be hoped for with a constant-gain algorithm is convergence to a situation in which beliefs eventually spend most of their time within a neighborhood (whose size depends on the gain parameter) of rational expectations beliefs.[10]

We display the results of using the constant-gain learning scheme in Figures 5 and 6. Evidently, convergence with a constant-gain algorithm occurs much faster in the economy with the simpler government policy (the one with government expen-

---

[10] See Evans and Honkapohja (1993b) for a discussion of some of the features of constant gain algorithms.

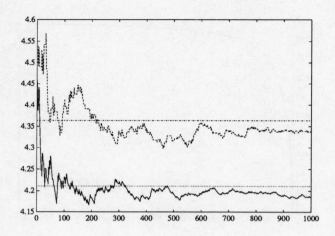

Figure 4. Simulation of saving rates of odd agents for stochastic approximation algorithm when $w_1 = 20, w_2 = 10, [G_1 \ G_2] = [0.8 \ 0], \pi = \begin{pmatrix} 0.75 & 0.25 \\ 0.5 & 0.5 \end{pmatrix}$. The rational expectations savings rates are 4.211, 4.364. The rational expectations rates of return on currency are $R = \begin{pmatrix} 0.81 & 1.0362 \\ 0.7817 & 1.00 \end{pmatrix}$. The dark line is the saving rate for state 1, the dotted line the saving rate for state 2. Also plotted are the rational expectations saving rates in states 1 and 2.

ditures always zero).

A comparison of the outcomes depicted in Figures 4 and 5 provides an idea of some of the tradeoffs involved between constant-gain and decreasing-gain algorithms.

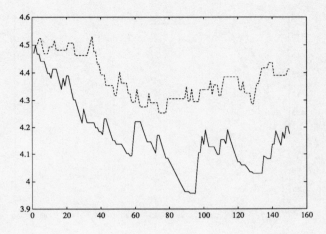

Figure 5. Simulation of saving rates for constant gain algorithm when $w_1 = 20, w_2 = 10, [G_1 \ G_2] = [0.8 \ 0], \pi = \begin{pmatrix} 0.75 & 0.25 \\ 0.5 & 0.5 \end{pmatrix}$. The gain γ is held constant at 0.05. The rational expectations savings rates are 4.211, 4.364. The rational expectations rates of return on currency are $R = \begin{pmatrix} 0.81 & 1.0362 \\ 0.7817 & 1.00 \end{pmatrix}$. The algorithm does not converge, but seems to get to the vicinity of the rational expectations saving rates. The savings rate for state 1 is shown in the solid line, that for state 2 in the dotted line.

Parametric and non-parametric adaptation

In the preceding formulation, people choose one saving rate for each level of government expenditure. This specification was designed potentially to let the system eventually 'learn' the rational expectations equilibrium, in which the 'state' is the $(n \times 1)$ vector G of government expenditures. By letting agents learn a distinct saving rate s to apply for each G, we are in effect letting them use a non-parametric specification to learn about a *policy function* $s = f(G)$.

There are two potential difficulties with this specification.

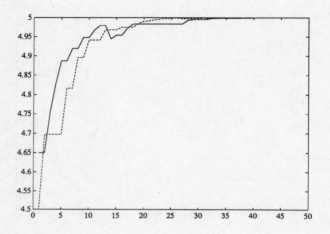

Figure 6. Simulation of saving rates for constant-gain algorithm when $\bar{G}_i = 0, i = 1, 2$. The gain is being held constant at 0.3 for each class of agents. Convergence is fast to the rational expectations savings rates.

First, the transition matrix π may imply that some states $\bar{G}_i$ are visited very infrequently. Observations from such states will roll in only slowly, making learning occur slowly. Of course, in terms of the *unconditional* expected utility of the agents, failure to learn about the correct thing to do in such infrequently visited states may cost little. Second, when the number of states n is large, the specification of one saving parameter for each state will become burdensome, again because the observations per state will roll in slowly.

An econometrician's or statistician's solution to this problem would be to assume a parametric form for the saving function $s = f(G, \theta)$, where θ is a vector of parameters, of small dimension relative to n, and then to use all of the observations to estimate θ. A recursive algorithm for estimating the parameters

θ would use the gradient

$$\partial U / \partial \theta = U'(s) \partial f / \partial \theta,$$

and the Jacobian $\partial U^2 / \partial \theta^2$. A recursive algorithm would be

$$\theta_{\tau+1} = \theta_\tau - \gamma_\tau M_{\tau+1}^{-1} \partial U / \partial \theta_\tau$$
$$M_{\tau+1} = M_\tau + \gamma_\tau (\partial^2 U / \partial \theta_\tau^2 - M_\tau).$$

This algorithm uses each observation to estimate a more or less smooth function $f(G, \theta)$ to be used to determine savings.

Use of a parametric form $f(G, \theta)$ for the saving function raises the issue of *approximation*. Evidently a learning scheme that uses a parametric specification has a chance eventually of converging to a rational expectations equilibrium only if a rational expectations equilibrium can be supported by a saving function within the class of functions determined by $f(G, \theta)$. For many models, the chosen econometrically convenient function $f(G, \theta)$ will *not* be compatible with the functions determined by a rational expectations equilibrium. In these situations, a learning scheme based on a parametric specification will, if it converges, converge to an approximate rational expectations equilibrium.[11]

Learning the hard way

In the preceding model, learning occurs between *non-overlapping* generations of grandparents to grandchildren, with the grandchildren adjusting their grandparents' saving choice after observing the consequences of their grandparents' choice.[12] This

[11] See Marcet and Marshall (1992) and Sargent (1991). Also, see Kenneth Judd (1990, 1992) for descriptions of a variety of numerical methods for computing approximate equilibria.

[12] A byproduct of setting things up in this way is the alternation of turns between odd and even sets of agents. This 'two-population' feature of the learning algorithm duplicates or resembles the experimental environments of Marimon and Sunder (1992) and Arifovic (1993), to be discussed in the next chapter.

model requires little of agents in the way of 'theorizing,' at the cost of rendering their learning dependent on the behaviors and experiences of their predecessors.

When we extend the horizon beyond two periods, it becomes increasingly inconvenient to model learning in this way because we have to wait longer for the consequences of life-time savings behavior to be known. If we attribute some 'theorizing' to our agents, we can avoid the need to learn only from one's predecessors' complete life-time experiences.

Learning via model formation

To motivate an alternative model of learning in this environment, consider the Euler equation for a young agent's saving decision within a rational expectations equilibrium:

$$(8) \qquad u'(w_1 - s_i) = E_t(u'(w_2 + s_t R_t) R_t),$$

where the conditional expectation $E_t(\cdot)$ is over the equilibrium distribution of the rate of return on currency, $R_t = p_t/p_{t+1}$, conditional on the current value of the deficit G_t. As earlier, s_i is the saving rate when $G_t = \bar{G}_i$. One way to formulate the problem of learning is to suppose that there is a representative young agent within each generation who knows the utility function u and how to compute the derivative $u'(\cdot)$, but who does *not* know the distribution with respect to which the conditional expectation $E_t(\cdot)$ is to be computed in (8). To cope with this situation, the agent forms a model of the probablity distribution with respect to which $E_t(\cdot)$ is to be computed, and adopts an algorithm for updating this distribution as new data arrive. At each point in time, the agent uses this estimated model distribution as the distribution in (8), and uses (8) to determine s_i. Then the price level is determined as above, namely, by

$$p_t = H_{t-1}/(N s_t - G_t).$$

We describe two methods for modelling and updating the required distributions.

Updating histograms

Here the agent's model is created by simply forming *histograms* of *ex post* realized rates of return R_t, one for each of the possible realized values of G_t. When $G_t = \bar{G}_i$ is observed at time t, the young agent forms s_i by using that histogram to represent the conditional expectation in (8). Let $r_j, j = 1, \ldots, J(t,i)$, be the population of values of R_t that have been observed prior to t to follow the event $G_t = \bar{G}_i$, where $J(t,i)$ is the number of times the event $G_t = \bar{G}_i$ has occurred prior to time t. Then s_i is the value that solves

$$u'(w_1 - s_i) = \sum_{j=1}^{J(t,i)} u'(w_2 + s_i r_j) r_j / J(t,i).$$

As time passes, the histograms are updated.

A parametric model of conditional probablities

Here the agent adopts a parametric model of the conditional probabilities, namely,

$$\text{Prob}\,(R_t \leq R | G_t = \bar{G}_i) = F(R, \bar{G}_i, \theta_i).$$

At time t the agent has an estimate of the parameters of the distributions θ_{it}, and uses them to determine behavior via the following approximation to (8):

$$u'(w_1 - s_i) = \int_R u'(w_2 + s_i R)\, R\, dF(R, \bar{G}_i, \theta_{it}).$$

As data on (R_t, G_t) pairs flow in, the agent uses an adaptive algorithm to update his estimates of θ_{it}. For example, for each i, let the distribution be a two-parameter distribution determined by the first and second moment. Then the agent would update these parameters using the stochastic approximation algorithm

$$\mu_\tau = \mu_{\tau-1} + (1/\tau)(R_\tau - \mu_{\tau-1})$$
$$m_\tau = m_{\tau-1} + (1/\tau)(R_\tau^2 - m_{\tau-1}),$$

where there is a different 'clock' $\tau(t)$ for each event $G_t = \bar{G}_i$.

Approximate equilibria

When we adopt a learning scheme that restricts agents' decision rules to too small a class of functions, we cannot expect the economy with adaptively learning agents ever to converge to a rational expectations equilibrium. The most we can hope is that the learning economy might converge to an *approximate equilibrium*, a concept that is used by applied researchers interested in computing rational expectations equilibria. In this section, I briefly describe some of the connections between algorithms to compute approximate equilibria and economies populated by adaptively learning agents.

Computing an equilibrium of the model becomes more demanding as we expand the dimension of the state space. Suppose that we modify the previous model by assuming that government expenditures are determined by the continuous state Markov process with transition kernel

$$\text{Prob}\{G_{t+1} \leq G' | G_t = G\} = F(G', G).$$

All other aspects of the model remain unchanged. We conjecture an equilibrium saving function of the form $s_t = f(G_t)$, and use the equilibrium conditions to derive restrictions on this function. The household's first-order conditions evaluated at $s_t = f(G_t)$ can be written

$$u'(w_1 - f(G)) = E_t(u'(w_2 + f(G)R_t)R_t),$$

where $E_t(\cdot) = E(\cdot | G_t)$. The equilibrium condition and the government budget constraint imply $N f(G_t) - N f(G_{t-1})R_{t-1} = G_t$, which can be solved for R_{t-1}:

$$R_{t-1} = (N f(G_t) - G_t)/N f(G_{t-1}).$$

Substituting this into household's first-order condition gives

(13)
$$u'(w_1 - f(G_t)) = E_t\left[u'(w_2 + (Nf(G_{t+1}) - G_{t+1})/N) \times \frac{Nf(G_{t+1}) - G_{t+1}}{Nf(G_{t+1})}\right],$$

which is a functional equation in $f(G_t)$.

There exist a number of methods for solving a functional equation like (13) numerically. All of these methods replace the function $f(G)$ with a finite-parameter approximation $f(G, \theta)$, then find values of the parameters θ that come as close as possible to satisfying (13).[13]

Method of parameterized expectations

Here is how Albert Marcet's method of parameterized expectations can be used approximately to solve the functional equation (13). For convenience, write the right side of (13) as $E_t k(G_t, G_{t+1})$ where $k(G_t, G_{t+1}) = u'(w_2 + (Nf(G_{t+1}) - G_{t+1})/N)(Nf(G_{t+1}) - G_{t+1})/Nf(G_{t+1})$.[14]

1. Guess that the conditional expectation on the right side of (13) has a form $h(G_t, \theta)$. Pick a starting value of θ, call it θ_j for $j = 1$. Use this guess and (13) to solve for an initial saving function $s_t = f(G_t, \theta_j)$.
2. Use a random number generator to draw a realization of length T from the Markov process $F(G', G)$. Use this simulation and $f(G_t, \theta_j)$ to generate a realization of $k(G_t, G_{t+1})$. Then use this realization to compute the non-linear regression coefficients θ_{j+1} in the regression $E_t k(G_t, G_{t+1}) = h(G_t, \theta_{j+1})$.
3. Solve the first-order condition $u'(w_1 - s_t) = h(G_t, \theta_{j+1})$ for a new saving function $f(G_t, \theta_{j+1})$.
4. Iterate on steps 1–3 to convergence.

[13] See Kenneth Judd (1992) for a critical survey of and guide to such methods.
[14] See Marcet and Marshall (1992) for a formal analysis of the algorithm.

There is evidently a close connection between this method for equilibrium computation and the behavior of a system populated by adaptive agents. Indeed, we can reinterpret a recursive or 'on-line' version of this algorithm as a system with adaptive agents. Thus, a recursive version of the nonlinear least squares algorithm is

$$\theta_{t+1} = \theta_t + (1/t)R_{t+1}^{-1}\Big(k(G_t, G_{t+1}) - h(G_t, \theta_t)\Big)\nabla h(G_t, \theta_t)$$

$$R_{t+1} = R_t + (1/t)\Big((\nabla h(G_t, \theta_t))(\nabla h(G_t, \theta_t))' - R_t\Big),$$

where $\nabla h(G, \theta)$ is the gradient of h with respect to the parameters θ. Upon noting the resemblance between this algorithm and the learning scheme (13), it is understandable that Marcet proposed his equilibrium computation scheme as an outgrowth of earlier work on the dynamics of least squares learning systems.

Learning and equilibrium computation

Learning algorithms and equilibrium computation algorithms look like each other. Equilibrium computation algorithms often have interpretations as *centralized learning algorithms* whereby the model builder, acting in a role of 'social planner,' gropes for a set of pricing functions for markets and decision rules for agents that will satisfy all of the individual optimum conditions and market-clearing conditions. We have also seen that learning systems with boundedly rational agents sometimes have interpretations as *decentralized equilibrium computation* algorithms.

Recursive kernel density estimation

A continuous state (for G_t) specification in the present model is a convenient context for describing another way to formulate learning nonparametrically, namely, via recursive kernel estimators of a kind studied by Chen and White (1993). To describe their formulation, we first recall the nature of kernel estimators. Suppose that we have T observations x_t, $t = 1, \ldots, T$, on the

n-dimensional random vector x drawn from an unknown joint density $F(x)$. Let $K(x) : \mathbf{R}^n \to \mathbf{R}$ be a probability density for x, say a multivariate normal density. Then the kernel estimator of the density of x is

$$\hat{F}(x) = \frac{1}{T} \sum_{t=0}^{T} K \left(\frac{x - x_t}{h} \right),$$

where $h > 0$ is a fixed 'bandwidth' parameter.

Chen and White study a modified recursive version of such estimators. They let $\{h_t\}_{t=0}^{\infty}$ be a sequence of bandwidths with $h_t \searrow 0$, and $\hat{F}_0(x)$ be an arbitrary initial density. Then they construct the sequence $\{\hat{F}_t(x)\}$ of distributions via the stochastic approximation algorithm

$$\hat{F}_t(x) = \hat{F}_{t-1}(x) + \frac{1}{t} \left[K \left(\frac{x - x_t}{h_t} \right) - \hat{F}_{t-1}(x) \right].$$

For the present example, we could let $x_t = [R_t, G_t]'$. At time t, we would let behavior be determined by the solution of a version of (8) in which the conditional expectation on the right side is evaluated with respect to the conditional distribution for R_t conditional on G_t that can be deduced from the joint density $\hat{F}_{t-1}(x)$.[15]

Learning in a model of the exchange rate

We now study an environment for which the rational expectations equilibrium exchange rate is indeterminate, but we expel all rational agents and replace them with adaptive agents.[16] We endow these adaptive agents with learning algorithms and

---

[15] Chen and White (1992, 1993) have attained results on rates of convergence of such nonparametric estimators under assumptions permitting less feedback from agents' behavior to outcomes than the present example admits.

[16] The environment is the one studied by Kareken and Wallace (1981).

initial values for their decisions, which serve to render the exchange rate and all other endogenous variables determinate.[17] We want to study how the exchange rate behaves, and whether a ghost of indeterminacy still lurks.

The economy consists of a sequence of overlapping generations of two-period lived agents. There are two kinds of currency, available in supplies H_1 and H_2 that are fixed over time. At each date $t \geq 1$, there are born a constant number N of young agents who are endowed with w_1 units of a nonstorable consumption good when young, and w_2 units when old. A young agent makes two decisions. First, he chooses an amount s_t to save when young. Second, he chooses a fraction λ_t to allocate to currency 1, and allocates the remainder to currency 2. A time t the young agent's realized utility from those decisions will be

$$
(14) \quad
\begin{aligned}
U(s_t, \lambda_t) =& u(w_1 - s_t) \\
& + u(w_2 + \lambda_t s_t p_{1t}/p_{1t+1} + (1 - \lambda_t) s_t p_{2t}/p_{2t+1}),
\end{aligned}
$$

where p_{it} is the price level at time t in terms of currency i, and p_{it}/p_{it+1} is the gross rate of return on currency i. Here $u(\cdot)$ is an increasing and strictly concave function of consumption of the one good. In the examples below, we shall set $u(c) = \ln(c)$. We calculate the gradient

$$
\begin{aligned}
\partial U/\partial s_t =& - u'(w_1 - s_t) \\
& + u'(w_2 + \lambda_t s_t p_{1t}/p_{1t+1} + (1 - \lambda_t) s_t p_{2t}/p_{2t+1}) \\
& \times (\lambda_t p_{1t}/p_{1t+1} + (1 - \lambda_t) p_{2t}/p_{2t+1}) \\
\partial U/\partial \lambda_t =& u'(w_2 + \lambda_t s_t p_{1t}/p_{1t+1} + (1 - \lambda_t) s_t p_{2t}/p_{2t+1}) s_t \\
& \times (p_{1t}/p_{1t+1} - p_{2t}/p_{2t+1}).
\end{aligned}
$$

---

[17] See Calvo (1988) and Evans, Honkapohja, and Sargent (1993) for setups in which a fraction $1 - \mu$ of agents is rational, and a fraction μ is 'adaptive' in particular senses. Both of these contributions are concerned with studying how dynamics might differ from the rational expectations dynamics even with a very small μ.

We also use the elements of the matrix of second partials.[18]

For the purposes of studying learning, the economy consists of two subsequences of agents. Each subsequence is identified with a class of agents, whom we dub 'odd' and 'even.' As in the preceding model, we have two clocks $\tau(t)$, one for odd and the other for even agents, that count only two-period episodes used to evaluate realized utility. Let γ_τ be a sequence of positive numbers satisfying $\lim_{\tau \to \infty} \tau \gamma_\tau = 1$. The values of (s_τ, λ_τ) for each class of agents evolve according to the recursive algorithm

$$
(15) \quad
\begin{aligned}
\begin{bmatrix} s_{\tau+1} \\ \lambda_{\tau+1} \end{bmatrix} &= \begin{bmatrix} s_\tau \\ \lambda_\tau \end{bmatrix} - \gamma_\tau R_{\tau+1}^{-1} \begin{bmatrix} \partial U / \partial s_\tau \\ \partial U / \partial \lambda_\tau \end{bmatrix} \\
R_{\tau+1} &= R_\tau + \gamma_\tau \left[\begin{bmatrix} \partial^2 U / \partial s_\tau^2 & \partial U^2 / \partial s_\tau \partial \lambda_\tau \\ \partial U^2 / \partial \lambda_\tau \partial s_\tau & \partial U^2 / \partial \lambda_\tau^2 \end{bmatrix} - R_\tau \right]
\end{aligned}
$$

There are two realizations of this algorithm, one for the odd agents, the other for the even agents. Agents of each class thus learn from the utility experience only of previous agents of their

---

[18] These are given by

$$
\begin{aligned}
\partial^2 U / \partial s_t^2 &= u''(w_1 - s_t) \\
&\quad + u''(w_2 + \lambda_t s_t p_{1t}/p_{1t+1} + (1 - \lambda_t)s_t p_{2t}/p_{2t+1}) \\
&\quad \times (\lambda_t p_{1t}/p_{1t+1} + (1 - \lambda_t)p_{2t}/p_{2t+1})^2 \\
\partial^2 U / \partial \lambda_t^2 &= u''(w_2 + \lambda_t s_t p_{1t}/p_{1t+1} + (1 - \lambda_t)s_t p_{2t}/p_{2t+1}) \\
&\quad \times s_t (p_{1t}/p_{1t+1} - p_{2t}/p_{2t+1})^2 \\
\partial^2 U / (\partial \lambda_t \partial s_t) &= u''(w_2 + \lambda_t s_t p_{1t}/p_{1t+1} + (1 - \lambda_t)s_t p_{2t}/p_{2t+1})s_t \\
&\quad \times (p_{1t}/p_{1t+1} - p_{2t}/p_{2t+1})(\lambda_t p_{1t}/p_{1t+1} + (1 - \lambda_t)p_{2t}/p_{2t+1}) \\
&\quad + u'(w_2 + \lambda_t s_t p_{1t}/p_{1t+1} + (1 - \lambda_t)s_t p_{2t}/p_{2t+1}) \\
&\quad \times (p_{1t}/p_{1t+1} - p_{2t}/p_{2t+1})
\end{aligned}
$$

own class.[19] The price level is determined by

(16)
$$p_{1t} = H_1/(\lambda_t s_t)$$
$$p_{2t} = H_2/((1 - \lambda_t)s_t).$$

In odd periods, the (s_t, λ_t) pair for the odd agents is used in (16), while in even periods, the (s_t, λ_t) pair for even agents is used in (16) to determine price levels in terms of the two currencies.

Given initial conditions for $(R_{t-1}, s_t, \lambda_t)$ for each class of agents, equations (14), (15), (16) determine the evolution of the decisions λ_t, s_t and the prices p_{it} in terms of the two currencies. The exchange rate is just p_{1t}/p_{2t}.

Figures 7 and 8 report the results of simulating this system starting from two different sets of initial conditions for (s, λ), but common initial conditions for the R's.[20] For each experiment, the exchange rate path rapidly converges to a constant value, but the limiting exchange rate values differ between the two economies. Evidently, the exchange rate depends sensitively on the initial conditions that we choose. Figure 9 shows saving rates for the two types of agents in experiment 1, while Figure 10 displays the evolution of their portfolio parameters λ. All of these parameters are gradually converging to values consistent with a rational expectations equilibrium.

---

[19] Algorithm (15) can be modified to incorporate 'simulated annealing' by replacing γ_t by $\gamma_\tau^* = (1 + \zeta_\tau)\gamma_\tau$ everywhere in the algorithm, where ζ_t is a random variable with mean zero. We can implement a so-called 'constant-gain' algorithm by setting $\gamma_t = \gamma_0$, a constant. A constant-gain algorithm with $\gamma_t = 1$ and with the initial value of R set equal to the Hessian implements Newton-Raphson.

[20] We set the parameters of the model at $w_1 = 20, w_2 = 15, H_1 = 100, H_2 = 120$.

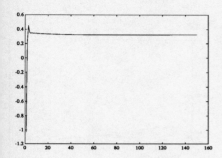

Figure 7. Logarithm of exchange rate in experiment 1.

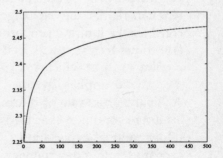

Figure 8. Logarithm of exchange rate for experiment 2. Experiments 1 and 2 share identical parameters, except for the initial conditions on λ for odd and even agents.

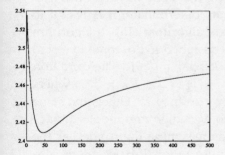

Figure 9a. Saving rate for odd agents in experiment 1.

Figure 9b. Saving rate for even agents in experiment 1.

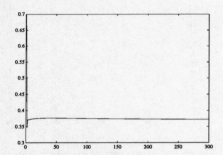

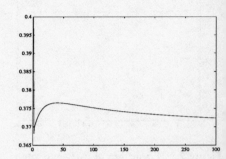

Figure 10a. λ for odd agents in
experiment 1.

Figure 10b. λ for even agents in
experiment 1.

Exchange rate initial-condition dependence

For the purpose of understanding the sense in which this system can render the exchange rate determinate, it is useful to
consider the limiting properties of algorithm (15). If algorithm
(15) comes to rest, it will, as it is designed to do, come to rest at
a point (λ, s) at which $[\partial U/\partial s \; \partial U/\partial \lambda] = [0\ 0]$. The condition
$\partial U/\partial \lambda = 0$ implies $p_{1t}/p_{1t+1} = p_{2t}/p_{2t+1}$, or $R_{1t} = R_{2t}$, where
R_{it} is the gross rate of return on currency i. This is the same
arbitrage condition that leads to exchange rate indeterminacy
under rational expectations. The reasoning that underlies the
exchange rate indeterminacy under rational expectations also
implies that the rest points of algorithm (15) leave the exchange
rate unrestricted. Our learning system renders the exchange
rate path determinate by having the 'dead hand of history' put
enough sluggishness into decisions. The exchange rate path can
be said to be 'history-dependent' because the initial conditions
assigned to (λ, s) assume an importance that does not vanish as

time passes.[21],[22]

The no-trade theorem

Jean Tirole (1982) proved a sharp 'no-trade' theorem that characterizes rational expectations equilibria in a class of models of purely speculative trading.[23],[24] The equilibrium market price fully reveals everybody's private information at zero trades for all traders. The no-trade theorem overrules the common-sense intuition that differences in information are a source of trading volume.

The remarkable no-trade outcome works the rational expectations hypothesis very hard. This is revealed clearly in Tirole's proof, which exploits elementary properties of the (commonly believed) probability distribution function determined by a rational expectations equilibrium. In this section, I describe how backing off rationality can (temporarily) undo the no-trade result, and produce a model of trading volume. I first describe an environment for which the no-trade theorem holds under rational expectations, then withdraw Tirole's rational agents and replace them with Robbins–Monro adaptive agents.

---

[21] It is possible to construct stochastic versions of this model in which the exchange rate is *path-dependent* in the sense that realizations emanating from identical initial conditions would eventually converge to different exchange rates because of the different realizations of the random processes impinging on the system's transient dynamics.

[22] Evans and Honkapohja (1993) describe how adaptive learning rules resolve equilibrium indeterminacy problems: 'models with multiple solutions are converted into models with path dependence in which the trajectory of the economy, and the [rational expectations equilibrium] attained in the limit, are determined through a learning rule by initial forecasts and by the sequence of exogenous shocks.'

[23] 'Purely speculative trading' means that all insurance and consumption-smoothing reasons for trading are assumed absent.

[24] Milgrom and Stokey describe a related no-trade theorem.

The environment

The environment is one analyzed in detail by John Hussman (1992).[25] There is a competitive market for a stock that is a claim on a dividend process $\{d_t\}$ governed by

(17a)
$$d_t = \theta_{1t} + \theta_{2t} + \epsilon_t$$
$$\theta_{1t} = \rho_1 \theta_{1t-1} + \nu_{1t}$$
$$\theta_{2t} = \rho_2 \theta_{2t-1} + \nu_{2t}$$

where $|\rho_1| < 1, |\rho_2| < 1$, and $[\epsilon_t \; \nu_{1t} \; \nu_{2t}]$ is a vector white noise. There are two classes of traders, dubbed a and b, present in equal numbers (for convenience we'll assume one each) who have different information about dividends. At time t, traders of both classes observe the history of the publicly available information $\{p_s, d_s; \; s \leq t\}$. In addition, traders of classes a and b, respectively, observe the pieces of 'private information':

(17b)
$$s_t^a = \theta_{1t} + \eta_t^a$$
$$s_t^b = \theta_{2t} + \eta_t^b$$

where (η_t^a, η_t^b) are white noises that are orthogonal to each other and to each component of $[\epsilon_t \; \nu_{1t} \; \nu_{2t}]$. At time t, traders of class j observe a history generated by the information vector $z_{jt} = [p_t \; s_t^j \; d_t]'$.

Traders behave myopically, each period maximizing the one-period utility function

$$E(-\exp(-W_{t+1}^j/\phi)) \mid I_{jt}, \quad \phi > 0,$$

subject to

$$W_{t+1}^j = RW_t^j + q_t^j(p_{t+1} + d_{t+1} - Rp_t),$$

where R is a constant gross interest rate on a risk-free asset, I_{jt} is agent j's information set, and q_t^j is agent j's purchases. This

---

[25] Hussman's work is related to work by Jiang Wang (1990). For other work on methods of circumventing the no trade theorem, see Harald Uhlig (1992).

leads to a demand function for trader of class j that is linear in the expected 'excess return':

$$(18) \qquad q_t^j = \phi_j E(p_{t+1} + d_{t+1} - Rp_t) \mid I_{jt}$$

where $\phi_j = \phi/\sigma^2_{p_{t+1}+d_{t+1}|I_{tj}}$; $\sigma^2_{p_{t+1}+d_{t+1}|I_{jt}}$ is the variance of $p_{t+1} + d_{t+1}$ conditional on the information set I_{jt}; and $(p_{t+1}+d_{t+1} - Rp_t)$ is the excess return of the stock over the risk-free asset.

Following Tirole, we assume that the asset is available in fixed supply $\bar{q}$, which for convenience we assume to be zero.[26] A rational expectations equilibrium is a stochastic process for $\{p_t\}$ that satisfies the market-clearing condition

$$(19) \qquad q_t^a + q_t^b = 0.$$

Prices fully revealing with no trade

For ease of exposition, we shall assume that in forming conditional expectations, agents of both classes condition only on the most recent observation z_{jt}, which means that we set $I_{jt} = z_{jt}$. Hussman (1992) and Sargent (1991) describe how to set things up to condition on the (infinite) history of z_{jt}. We also replace conditional expectations with linear regressions, a step we can defend by one of two standard justifications.[27] Substituting the demand functions (18) into equilibrium condition (19) gives[28]

$$\phi_a E(y_t \mid z_{at}) + \phi_b E(y_t \mid z_{bt}) = 0$$

or

$$(20) \qquad E(y_t \mid z_{at}) = -\frac{\phi_b}{\phi_a} E(y_t \mid z_{bt})$$

---

[26] The important thing is that the supply is fixed over time.

[27] Either assume that all distributions are multivariate normal or restrict decision rules to be linear.

[28] Models with 'noise traders' break the no-trade theorem by replacing (19) with $q_t^a + q_t^b = \zeta_t$, where $\{\zeta_t\}$ is an exogenous stochastic process of supplies by the noise traders. Technically, notice how the presence of a time-varying, random $\{\zeta_t\}$ process disrupts the argument leading to (20).

where the random variable $y_t = (p_{t+1} + d_{t+1} - Rp_t)$ measures the excess return of the stock over the risk-free asset. Writing the regressions $E(y_t \mid z_{jt}) = \delta_j z_{jt}$, (20) implies

$$(21) \qquad \delta_a z_{at} = \frac{-\phi_b}{\phi_a} \delta_b z_{bt}.$$

Because we have assumed that the information vector $z_{at} \neq z_{bt}$, (21) can hold $\forall\, t$ only if both sides are constant over time. However, (20) with $E(y_t \mid z_{at}) = \alpha$, α a constant implies $E(y_t \mid z_{at}) = E(y_t \mid z_{bt}) = 0.$[29] Substituting $Ey_t | z_{jt}$ into the demand functions shows the no-trade outcome. The condition that $Ey_t | I_{jt} = 0 \,\forall\, j$ shows that the market price adjusts to reveal fully all of the private information that is relevant for predicting excess returns.

Computation of the equilibrium

In order both to study the rational expectations equilibrium in more detail and to provide a framework from which we can expel rational agents and resettle adaptive agents, it is useful to have a way of computing the rational expectations equilibrium. We follow Hussman and adapt the apparatus of Marcet and Sargent (1989b) to this purpose. A trader of type j observes the history of $z_{jt} = [\, p_t \quad s_t^j \quad d_t \,]'$, fits the vector autoregression,[30]

$$(22) \qquad z_{jt} = \beta_j z_{jt-1} + \zeta_{jt},$$

and uses it to forecast the components of z_{jt}:

$$E z_{jt+1} \mid z_{jt} = \beta_j z_{jt}.$$

Then trader j's estimate of excess returns $(p_{t+1} + d_{t+1} - Rp_t) = y_t$ is

$$(23) \qquad E(y_t \mid z_{jt}) = \delta_j z_{jt}$$

---

[29] Applying the law of iterated expectations to (20), and noting that $E(E(y_t \mid z_{at})) = E(E(y_t \mid z_{bt})) = \alpha$, implies $(1 + \phi_b/\phi_a)\alpha = 0$, or $\alpha = 0$.
[30] The vector ζ_{jt} is the innovation vector.

where $\delta_j = [1\ 0\ 1]\,\beta_j + [-R\ 0\ 0]$.

The state vector and the innovation vector for the market are

$$z_t = \begin{bmatrix} p_t \\ s_t^a \\ s_t^b \\ d_t \\ \theta_{1t} \\ \theta_{2t} \end{bmatrix}, \quad u_t = \begin{bmatrix} \eta_t^a \\ \eta_t^b \\ \nu_{1t} \\ \nu_{2t} \\ \epsilon_t \end{bmatrix}$$

Using (23) and the equilibrium condition (19), we can derive a state transition equation of the form

$$(24) \qquad z_t = T(\beta)z_{t-1} + V(\beta)u_t,$$

where $T(\beta), V(\beta)$ are matrix functions of $\beta = (\beta_a, \beta_b)$ that are described by Hussman. The form of (24) emphasizes how traders' perceptions of the laws of motion, as parameterized by the vector autoregressive parameters β_j, influence the law of motion for the entire state z_t.

Since z_{jt} is a subvector of z_t, system (24) can be used to deduce the projections

$$(25) \qquad E(z_{jt} \mid z_{jt-1}) = S_j(\beta)z_{jt-1},$$

where $S_j(\beta)$ depends on $(T(\beta), V(\beta))$ and the moments $E\,u_t u_t'$. Thus, we have a mapping from a pair of perceived laws of motion $\beta = (\beta_a, \beta_b)$ to a pair of matrices $(S_a(\beta),\ S_b(\beta))$ that determine optimal (linear least squares) predictors. A rational expectations equilibrium is a fixed point of this mapping.

Tampering with the no-trade theorem

The no-trade theorem follows directly from the equality

$$(26) \qquad \phi_a \delta_a z_{at} + \phi_b \delta_b z_{bt} = 0,$$

and in particular from the facts that δ_j, $j = a, b$ are each constant over time, and that $\delta_j z_{jt}$, $j = a, b$ are each a conditional expectation of the same random variable, conditioned on different information sets, but calculated with respect to the same joint probability distribution. We can temporarily disrupt the forces leading to the no-trade theorem by withdrawing from our agents knowledge of the (equilibrium) joint probability distributions required to compute $E(y_t \mid z_{jt})$, and giving them instead initial conditions for β_j in their vector autoregressions and a recursive algorithm for updating their estimates of β_j.[31] The effect of this will be to replace (26) with an equilibrium condition of the form

$$(27) \qquad \phi_a \delta_{at} z_{at} + \phi_b \delta_{bt} z_{bt} = 0,$$

where $\delta_{jt} = [1\ 0\ 1]\ \beta_{jt} + [-R\ 0\ 0]$. The facts that δ_{jt} in (27) are time-dependent, and that they start from arbitrary initial conditions, raises the possibility that $\delta_{at} z_{at} \neq \delta_{bt} z_{bt}$, so that trade will occur.

The system's motion is described by

$$z_t = T(\beta_{t-1}) z_{t-1} + V(\beta_{t-1}) u_t$$
$$M_{jt} = M_{jt-1} + (1/t)\,(z_{jt-1} z'_{jt-1} - M_{jt-1})$$
$$\beta'_{jt} = \beta'_{jt-1} + (1/t)\,M_{jt}^{-1} z_{jt-1}(z_{jt} - \beta_{jt-1} z_{jt-1})'$$

where $\beta_t = (\beta_{at}, \beta_{bt})$, and the first equation is formed simply by replacing β by β_{t-1} in (24). To start the system, we need initial conditions for (β_j, M_j) for $j = a, b$. We shall start the system from initial conditions in the vicinity of a rational expectations equilibrium.

Some experiments

Figures 11, 12, and 13 report some simulations of the system with least squares learning.[32] Figure 11 plots the price and volume from a simulation of a system with least squares learning,

---

[31] The work described in this section is from Hussman and Sargent (1993).

[32] Parameter values were set at $\rho_1 = 0.8, \rho_2 = 0.4, \phi = 1, R = 1.1, E u_t u'_t = I$. I have omitted constants from the dividend process, with the consequence that equilibrium prices fluctuate around zero. By adding constants, we could make prices fluctuate around a positive number.

where the system has been initiated with beliefs that are per-
turbed by very small amounts from the rational expectations
beliefs, and the covariance matrixes (the M_j's) have been set
close to those from the asymptotic distribution theory that governs the regression of someone who had lived for 100 periods
in the rational expectations equilibrium. These graphs illustrate
how the price with least squares learning resembles the rational expectations price, but diverges enough from it to generate
volume. Hussman and Sargent studied the behavior of such
systems over much longer horizons, and found that over time
the gap between the rational expectations price and the price
under least squares learning vanishes, and so does volume. But
positive trading volume persists for a very long time.

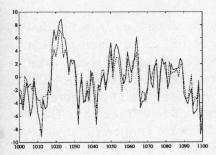 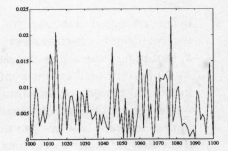

Figure 11a. Rational expectations price (solid
line) and price under least squares learning
(dotted line) after 1000 periods of learning,
with initial beliefs close to those appropriate
for a rational expectations equilibrium.

Figure 11b. Volume with least squares learning after 1000 periods.

Figures 12 and 13 plot parts of a simulation of the same model
with initial beliefs that assign too much weight to the market
price in determining expected excess return. In particular, initial

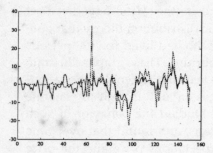
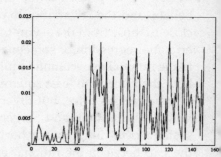

Figure 12a. Rational expectations price (solid line) and price under least squares learning (dotted line), starting from beliefs that overweight the market price: first 150 observations.

Figure 12b. Volume under least squares learning, starting from beliefs that overweight the market price.

beliefs are equal to the rational expectations beliefs except that the coefficients on current price in the vector autoregression determining expected excess return are raised in absolute value by 40 percent *vis à vis* their rational expectations values. The initial 150 periods of the simulation are plotted in Figure 12, while Figure 13 plots observations after 1000 periods. These figures indicate how we can make prices temporarily diverge from their rational expectations values by driving initial beliefs farther away from the rational expectations values. Figure 13 shows how, with the passage of time, least squares beliefs are adapting to eliminate differences from rational expectations.[33]

Sustaining volume with a constant gain

We can prevent convergence to rational expectations and extinction of volume by assigning agents constant-gain (i.e., $\gamma_t = $

[33] The price differences show higher-than-normal kurtosis, which decreases toward three as the system converges to a rational expectations equilibrium.

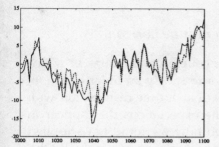

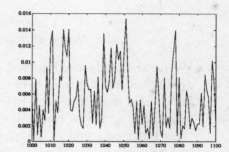

Figure 13a. Rational expectations price (solid line) and price under least squares learning (dotted line), starting from beliefs that over-weight the market price, after 1000 periods of learning.

Figure 13b. Volume under least squares learning, starting from beliefs that overweight the market price, after 1000 periods of learning.

$\gamma^* > 0$) versions of the recursive algorithm. By setting γ^*, we can control the neighborhood of a rational expectations equilibrium, and the average level of volume to which this model would eventually converge.

Using a constant-gain algorithm might be a good idea for agents who take time invariance of their forecasting model with a grain of salt, and who place a premium on adaptability.[34] Constant-gain algorithms assign enough greater weight to recent observations than ordinary least squares to defeat the forces that generate consistency of ordinary least squares under classical conditions. The stay-on-your-toes spirit of constant-gain algorithms can have advantages in situations (like this no-trade model with least squares learning) in which one is fitting a time-invariant model where the law of motion is really time-varying.

---

[34] In the model of Sims and Chung to be described in Chapter 7, we shall see a situation in which using a 'random coefficients' specification enhances a government policy-maker's adpatability and sometimes leads to superior outcomes, relative to those implied by 'decreasing-gain' specifications.

In giving up the ability to converge, the constant-gain adapter retains an ability to keep up with the times.[35]

Learning with an infinite horizon

We have already encountered a couple of situations in which agents want to set their behavior to satisfy an Euler equation, and where they only need to learn about the distribution with respect to which to compute the expectations that appear in their Euler equation. I described how we could have applied this setup to the Markov deficit example, and we actually did the no-trade example in this way. In those examples, because of the short horizons of the agents, there were alternative ways to model learning, e.g. by letting agents 'learn the hard way' by observing the past utility-experiences associated with the dynamic plans of their predecessors. Where agents have infinite planning horizons, we are more restricted in how we can model agents' learning.

To illustrate learning (with coaxing) in a simple infinite-horizon context, this section describes least squares learning in the context of a linear version of Lucas and Prescott's equilibrium model of investment under uncertainty, an example studied by Marcet and Sargent (1989a). This example has the following features:

(a) Because the horizon is infinite, agents in the model get a lot of coaxing. The model is set up so that agents know most of what they require to make optimal decisions, and only

---

[35] There are alternative ways to break the no-trade theorem. One class of alternatives would alter the environment to restore non-speculative motives for asset trades, e.g. via endowment heterogeneity coupled with consumption smoothing motives. Another class of explanations would retain the only-speculative motive assumption, but would model trading processes explicitly in such a way that positive volume and lack of full revelation of information would be the outcome of implementing one of the auction mechanisms analyzed, say, by Gresik and Satterthwaite (1989). I don't know whether the learning route described in the text is more promising than these alternatives.

learn about a limited aspect of the system, namely, the law of motion involving an aggregate endogenous state variable. Firms know enough to form and solve their Euler equation, but don't know the equilibrium conditional distribution of the future values of the output prices that appear on the right side. Firms use a recursively updated estimate of a vector autoregression to solve their Euler equation.

(b) Verifying the convergence of the system is technically difficult because the firms are learning about a 'moving target,' a law of motion that is influenced by their own learning behavior.

Investment under uncertainty

A representative firm chooses its capital stock k_t to maximize

$$(28) \qquad E \sum_{t=0}^{\infty} \delta^t (p_t f k_t - (d/2)(k_t - k_{t-1})^2),$$

where $\delta \in (0,1)$, $f > 0, d > 0$, and where p_t is the price of a single commodity. The price of the commodity is determined in a competitive market. The demand for the commodity is governed by

$$(29) \qquad p_t = A_0 - A_1 f K_t + u_t,$$

where K_t is the average level of capital used to produce output in this market (so that average output is $f K_t$), and $\{u_t\}$ is a serially uncorrelated random process with mean zero. Under rational expectations, the firm is supposed to know the law of motion for average capital, namely,

$$(30) \qquad K_t = \beta_0 + \beta_1 K_{t-1} + v u_t,$$

and to use it in conjunction with (29) to forecast prices. Under the assumption that the firm knows the laws (29), (30) governing prices and the market-wide average capital stock, the

firm's problem can be represented as a dynamic programming
or discrete-time calculus of variations problem. The Euler equation associated with this problem is

$$(31) \qquad k_t = k_{t-1} + (f/d)E_t \sum_{j=0}^{\infty} \delta^j p_{t+j},$$

where E_t is the conditional expectation evaluated with respect
to the equilibrium distribution generated by (29), (30).

Rational expectations equilibrium as a fixed point

For given values of β_0, β_1 in (29), the prediction problem associated with the right side of the Euler equation (31) can be
formulated as follows. Represent (30) as

$$\begin{bmatrix} K_{t+1} \\ 1 \end{bmatrix} = \begin{bmatrix} \beta_1 & \beta_0 \\ 0 & 1 \end{bmatrix} \begin{bmatrix} K_t \\ 1 \end{bmatrix} + \begin{bmatrix} v \\ 0 \end{bmatrix} u_{t+1},$$

or

$$(32) \qquad x_{t+1} = \beta x_t + \begin{bmatrix} v \\ 0 \end{bmatrix} u_{t+1},$$

where $x_t = [\, K_t \quad 1\,]'$. Using (32) to evaluate the conditional
expectation, the Euler equation can be represented as

$$k_t = k_{t-1} + (f/d(1-\delta))A_0 + (f/d)u_t$$
$$(33) \qquad\qquad - [\,1 \quad 0\,](A_1 f^2/d)(I - \delta\beta)^{-1} \begin{bmatrix} K_t \\ 1 \end{bmatrix}.$$

Equation (33) summarizes individual firm behavior under the
beliefs (30) about the aggregate state K_t. We impose equilibrium
by setting $k_t = K_t$, and solving the resulting equation for the
actual law of motion for K_t induced by the beliefs (30). We
obtain

$$(34) \qquad K_t = T_1(\beta_1)K_{t-1} + T_0(\beta) + V(\beta_1)u_t,$$

where

$$T_1(\beta_1) = \frac{(1 - \delta\beta_1)}{1 - \delta\beta_1 + A_1 f^2/d}$$

$$T_0(\beta) = \left[f/(d(1 - \delta))A_0 - (A_1 f^2 \delta\beta_0)/(d(1 - \delta)(1 - \delta\beta_1)) \right] T_1(\beta_1)$$

This construction induces a mapping from a perceived law of motion for K_t into an actual one. When firms *believe* that the law of motion is (30), they act to make the actual law of motion (34). A rational expectations equilibrium is a fixed point of this mapping, namely, a pair β_0, β_1 that satisfy

$$\beta_0 = T_0(\beta)$$
$$\beta_1 = T_1(\beta_1).$$

Least squares learning

Marcet and Sargent (1989a) describe a version of this model with adaptive agents. Firms formulate and recursively estimate an autoregression of the form (30), using the stochastic approximation algorithm

(35)
$$\beta'_t = \beta'_{t-1} - (1/t)R_t^{-1}(x_{t-2}(\beta_{t-1}x_{t-2} - x_{t-1})')$$
$$R_t = R_{t-1} + (1/t)(x_{t-1}x'_{t-1} - R_{t-1}).$$

Firms' behavior is determined each period by using the *estimated* vector autoregression to evaluate the conditional expectation on the right side of the Euler equation (30). This behavior causes the actual evolution of the capital stock to be

(36)
$$K_t = T_1(\beta_t)K_{t-1} + T_0(\beta_t) + V(\beta_t)u_t.$$

Technically, this example has many of the features of Bray's model, with the additional feature that, even in the rational expectations equilibrium (i.e. the system without learning), there is a state variable, K_t, that imparts dynamics to the system.

It is about the law of motion of that state variable, and not a fixed mean, that the firms are learning. Nevertheless, very similar considerations govern the convergence of this system to a rational expectations equilibrium.

Marcet and Sargent (1989a) applied methods developed by Lennart Ljung (1977) to describe the sense in which the limiting behavior of the stochastic difference equations (35), (36) is governed by the associated ordinary differential equations

(37)
$$\frac{d}{dt} \begin{pmatrix} \beta_1 \\ \beta_0 \end{pmatrix} = R^{-1} M_x(\beta) \begin{bmatrix} T_1(\beta) - \beta_1 \\ T_0(\beta) - \beta_0 \end{bmatrix}$$

$$\frac{d}{dt} R = M_x(\beta) - R,$$

where $M_x(\beta) = E x_t x_t'$, from system (34), evaluated at the fixed vector β. Notice that the rest points of this system are rational expectations equilibria. Stability of this ordinary differential equation system about the rational expectations equilibrium is a necessary condition for the (almost sure) convergence of the stochastic difference equations (35), (36) to the rational expectations equilibrium. Sufficiency is more tenuous and troublesome.[36],[37] Marcet and Sargent studied the technical complications that the presence of learning about a law of motion for an endogenous state variable like K_t added to the sort of system studied by Bray.

---

[36] The sufficient conditions for convergence that have been discovered to date involve adding some side conditions to the least squares algorithm designed to insure that the altered algorithm visits the basin of attraction of the fixed point of the operator $T(\beta)$ infinitely often.

[37] Marcet and Sargent also study the sense in which the *local* stability of the learning scheme is governed by the smaller o.d.e.

$$\frac{d}{dt} \begin{pmatrix} \beta_1 \\ \beta_0 \end{pmatrix} = \begin{bmatrix} T_1(\beta) - \beta_1 \\ T_0(\beta) - \beta_0 \end{bmatrix}.$$

Convergence theorems

I now briefly describe a method that has been used to analyze the limiting properties of models in which the agents' behavior is determined by their use of adaptive estimators.[38] Such systems have the property that laws of evolution of the endogenous variables are determined in part by the adaptive estimation process. Because the agents are learning about a system that is being influenced by the learning processes of people like themselves, these systems are sometimes called 'self-referential.' That the adaptive estimators are not estimating the parameters of a fixed data-generating mechanism means that standard econometric proofs of convergence of estimators (e.g., their consistency and asymptotic efficiency) cannot usually be applied. Instead, another approach based on stochastic approximation methods has increasingly been used.

I shall illustrate the kind of analysis that can be done with stochastic approximation methods in the context of a particular example, namely our model with a stochastic government deficit.[39] Consider a version of that model in which agents are learning via a parametric model which they fit to the distribution of the return on currency. In particular, assume that agents generate forecasts of the rate of return on currency by fitting the parametric model

$$(38) \qquad \bar{E}_t R_t = f(G_t; \theta_t),$$

where θ_t is the time t estimate of the vector of parameters θ in the probability model, and $f(\cdot; \theta)$ is a possibly nonlinear function mapping the government deficit G into a forecast of the

[38] This section is based on Marcet and Sargent (1989a) and Woodford (1990).

[39] Bullard and Duffy (1993) study least squares learning in an economy with overlapping generations of n-period lived agents. For $n \geq 4$, they find that least squares learning *fails* to converge locally to a rational expectations equilibrium. Also see Bullard (1991) for a discussion of how complicated nonlinear dynamics can sometimes emerge out of least squares learning.

rate of return on currency between t and $t + 1$, which we denote $\bar{E}_t R_t$. We assume that agents use the following stochastic approximation algorithm for estimating θ_t:

(39)
$$\theta_{t+1} = \theta_t + (1/t)M_t^{-1}(\nabla f_t)(R_t - f(G_t; \theta_t))$$
$$M_{t+1} = M_t + (1/t)((\nabla f_t)(\nabla f_t)' - M_t),$$

where ∇f_t is the gradient of f with respect to θ evaluated at θ_t and G_t. Recall that (39) simply implements a recursive nonlinear least squares algorithm.

The model has the self-referential property that, when agents forecast according to the rule (38) and when the θ's are updated according to (39), the *optimal* forecast has a form

$$E_t R_t = h(G_t),$$

where

(40)
$$R_t = h(G_t) + u_t,$$

where E_t is the conditional expectation operator, $h(\cdot)$ is a function mapping G_t into the least squares forecast $E_t R_t$, and $\{u_t\}$ is a random process with the property that u_t is orthogonal to *every* (Borel measurable) function of G_t.[40] The function $h(G)$, which depends on (θ_t, M_t), is determined implicitly by the process of solving the model.[41]

Substituting (40) into (39), the recursive learning algorithm can be written

(41)
$$\theta_{t+1} = \theta_t + (1/t)M_t^{-1}(\nabla f_t)(h(G_t) + u_t - f(G_t; \theta_t))$$
$$M_{t+1} = M_t + (1/t)((\nabla f_t)(\nabla f_t)' - M_t).$$

---

[40] This property of u_t identifies $h(\cdot)$ as the conditional expectation function.

[41] The function h is understood to embed the dependence of θ_{t+1} on θ_t, M_t via equation (39). The price level p_{t+1} depends on θ_{t+1} because θ_{t+1} influences savings behavior at $t + 1$.

An associated ordinary differential equation

We want to study the behavior of the system formed by the assumed exogenous Markov process for government expenditures G which together with equations (40) and (41) determines the evolution of $(G_t, R_t, \theta_t, M_t)$. In particular, we want to find some conditions under which this system converges to an asymptotically stationary system in which the parameters determining beliefs (θ, M) stop moving. When convergence does occur, we want to describe the resulting limit point in terms of how it relates to the concept of a rational expectations equilibrium.

Application of arguments in the spirit of Ljung and Söderström (1983) and Kushner and Clark (1978) can be used to show that the limiting behavior of the system of stochastic difference equations defined by the Markov process for G and equations (40) and (41) is determined by an associated system of ordinary differential equations. This associated differential equation is derived by conducting the following mental experiment. Temporarily suspend the operation of system (41), and consider the system operating with a *fixed* θ for ever. Assume that *this* system converges to a unique invariant distribution,[42] and let $h^*(G_t) = T(\theta)(G_t)$ be the conditional expectation of R_t evaluated with respect to this invariant distribution. Form the associated differential equation system:

$$(42) \quad \begin{aligned} (d/dt)\theta &= E(M^{-1}\nabla f(T(\theta)(G) - f(G,\theta))) \\ (d/dt)M &= E((\nabla f)(\nabla f)') - M, \end{aligned}$$

where E is the unconditional expectation operator evaluated with respect to the asymptotic stationary distribution associated with the fixed parameter vector θ. The system of ordinary differential equations (42) is formed mechanically by taking expectations of the objects 'to the right of $(1/t)$' in equation system (41), and using the resulting expectations to estimate the average motion of (θ, M) over small intervals of time dt. The

---

[42] i.e., a unique asymptotic stationary distribution.

expectations are taken with respect to the stationary distribution associated with a fixed θ.[43]

We also consider the smaller ordinary differential equation system

(43) $$(d/dt)\theta = E((\nabla f)(T(\theta)(G) - f(G, \theta))).$$

Propositions

Several properties of systems like this have recurred in a variety of contexts, among the important ones being:

(a) The rest points of the ordinary differential equation (o.d.e) system (42) satisfy

(44)
$$E(\nabla f)(T(\theta)(G) - f(G, \theta)) = 0$$
$$E(\nabla f)(\nabla f)' = M.$$

If the support of $f(G, \theta)$ includes a rational expectations equilibrium, the first equation of (44) can be satisfied by $T(\theta)(G) - f(G, \theta) = 0$, in which case we have a rational expectations equilibrium as a rest point of (42) or (43). If the support of $f(G, \theta)$ does not include a rational expectations equilibrium, then the first equation of (44) identifies a set of *orthogonality conditions* that are the first-order necessary conditions for a special approximation problem. If the function $T(\theta)$ were independent of θ (which it usually is *not*), then these equations would be orthogonality conditions for the problem: find the value of θ which makes the function $f(G, \theta)$ best approximate the fixed function $T(G)$, where the approximation criterion is the mean square difference between the functions

$$E|T(\theta)(G) - f(\theta, G)|^2.$$

---

[43] Notice the 'mean field theory' flavor of this approach: approximating deterministic dynamics are being used to study aspects of an underlying stochastic process.

The approximation problem is unusual because θ determines the approximating function f and also influences the function being approximated $h^* = T(\theta)$. This aspect of the approximation problem reflects the self-referential property of the system.

(b) If the estimators (θ_t, M_t) converge, they converge to a rest point of the ordinary differential equation (42).

(c) If a fixed point of the ordinary differential equation (42) is locally unstable, then the estimator θ_t cannot converge to that fixed point.

(d) Suppose that the ordinary differential equation (42) is globally stable about a unique rest point. Then there exists a modification of the recursive algorithm for θ_t, M_t which converges almost surely to the rest point. [44]

(e) Convergence theorems require that $\{\gamma_t\}$ look like $\{1/t\}$. Convergence will not occur with 'constant-gain' versions of the algorithm. [45]

(f) Few results are available on *rates* of convergence. However, theorems described by Benveniste, Métivier, and Priouret (1990) can sometimes be used to show that a necessary and sufficient condition for $\sqrt{T}$-convergence of θ_t to the fixed point is that the eigenvalues of the Jacobian of the linear

---

[44] The modifications are devices that 'project' the estimator back into the intersection of the domain of attraction of the fixed point with the set of values of θ for which the system converges to an asymptotically stationary distribution for R_t, G_t. See Ljung (1977), Ljung and Söderström (1983), and Marcet and Sargent (1989a) for a discussion of various ways of modifying the algorithm. What is needed to get the stochastic approximation approach to yield almost sure convergence to a fixed point of the o.d.e. is some device that assures that the algorithm infinitely often visits the domain of attraction of the fixed point of the o.d.e.

[45] The most that can be hoped for with constant-gain versions of the algorithm is convergence in a stochastic sense of visiting a specified neighborhood of a fixed point of the o.d.e. with a relative frequency that depends, among other thing, on the gain parameter γ.

approximation to the small o.d.e. (43) at the fixed point are all less than $-1/2$ in modulus. Notice that this condition is stronger than the necessary condition for 'local stability' of the algorithm at the fixed point, namely that the eigenvalues of this same linear approximation are less than 0 in modulus. [46]

Propositions like (a), (b), (c), and (e) are not difficult to obtain, and can be expected to apply across a wide variety of models, both linear models like those studied by Marcet and Sargent (1989a, 1989b, 1992) and nonlinear ones like the ones studied by Woodford (1990). Propositions like (d) are harder to obtain, and often involve delicate and involved computations to verify assumptions sufficient to assure almost sure convergence. The amount of work to be done depends on the details of the device that is used to force the algorithm infinitely often into the domain of attraction of a fixed point. So far very little formal work has been done along the lines of proposition (f) about rates of convergence. [47]

Conclusions

The examples in this chapter all take an environment that had been studied under rational expectations and add a source of transient dynamics coming from adaptive least squares learning. The dynamics are transient because the 'fundamentals' in these environments are time-invariant, and because the adaptive algorithms we have given our boundedly rational agents eventually settle upon good time-invariant decision rules for those environments. [48]

---

[46] See Marcet and Sargent (1992) for an analysis of rates convergence in a particular model, with part of the analysis being based on the theorems of Benveniste *et al.*, and another part being based on Monte Carlo methods. Also see Ljung, Pflug, and Walk (1992).

[47] See Chung-Ming Kuan (1989) and Mohr (1990) for useful early contributions. Marcet and Sargent (1993) state a proposition about a rate of convergence.

[48] The exceptions are the constant-gain algorithms.

Are transient dynamics created in this way likely to be a useful addition to the list of ways that applied economists have of inducing dynamics? Among the principal mechanisms through which applied economists induce dynamics are:

(a) Capital (physical and human).

(b) Costs of adjustment.

(c) Serially correlated exogenous processes and disturbances.

(d) Information structures that induce agents to solve signal extraction problems or incentive problems.

I suspect that it is too early to add the sort of transient dynamics described in this chapter to this list of workhorses in applied economic dynamics. However, the examples in this chapter can teach us various things.

1. Beyond exhibiting the structure of a model of market equilibrium with dynamic supply behavior under least squares learning, Bray's model displays circumstances under which at least one class of plausible adaptive algorithms eventually converges to rational expectations.

2. The model with a stochastic government deficit sensitizes us to the issue that how fast adaptive agents can be expected to learn to have rational expectations depends on how complicated is the stochastic environment they must learn about, and how much prior information they are endowed with by way of a parametric form to learn about. In particular, how fast adaptive agents learn depends on how complicated is the government policy regime.

3. Adaptive algorithms are in principle capable of resolving indeterminacies in some rational expectations models like our exchange rate model, but in a very tenuous way. In our exchange rate example, the equations determining the limiting behavior of the system leave the exchange rate inde-

terminate (because those equations just recover the logic of exchange rate indeterminacy), but the adaptive algorithms assign enough force to initial conditions and to 'history' to determine the exchange rate path. By sufficiently tying down the expectations process that was left underdetermined by the rational expectations equilibrium, the adaptive mechanism selects an exchange rate path. This may seem a weak reed on which to base exchange rate determination.[49]

4. Adaptive learning provides enough friction temporarily to break the logic of the no-trade theorem, and so to provide a model of trading volume. This is one of a class of examples in which incorporating adaptive agents would serve, at least temporarily, to modify or take the edge off very sharp predictions that arise in some rational expectations models. One can imagine using similar shading of sharp rational expectations results in particular environments giving rise to Ricardian or Modigliani–Miller results for government monetary–fiscal operations.

5. A comparison of the Marcet–Sargent example with some of the earlier ones shows that there are many choices to be made in endowing our artificial agents with adaptive algorithms. These choices supply differing amounts of 'coaxing' to our boundedly rational agents.

In the next two chapters I shall describe more potential uses of models of bounded rationality.

---

[49] Put differently, a regime that allows the exchange rate to be history-dependent seems to be an ill-formed mechanism.

6
Experiments

Interpreting experiments

Arthur (1991) and Rust, Palmer, and Miller (1992) have used adaptive algorithms to mimic and interpret the behavior of human subjects in experiments. In this chapter we describe some experiments that have been performed on two models of monetary economies that appeared in earlier chapters. Among the goals of the experimenters was to shed light on the quality of guidance supplied by rational expectations and adaptive dynamics in selecting among multiple stationary equilibria. The first example is an overlapping-generations monetary economy with two stationary equilibria. The second is the exchange rate model with indeterminate equilibria.

A model of inflation

Marimon and Sunder (1992) put human subjects in an experiment designed to mimic a model with multiple equilibria that had been studied by Sargent and Wallace, Bruno and Fischer, and Marcet and Sargent.[1]

In this model, the 'rational expectations dynamics' and the 'adaptive dynamics' share common rest points but assign opposite stability characteristics to those rest points. Marimon and

---

[1] In addition to studying the stability of the two stationary equilibria under rational expectations and adaptive dynamics, Bruno and Fischer (1990) study how the existence of the 'bad Laffer curve' equilibrium can be precluded through choice of a monetary–fiscal policy operating rule.

Sunder's goal was to study how the experimental observations would match these different theoretical dynamics.

The environment

The model is a nonstochastic version of the overlapping-generations model with government expenditures described in the previous chapter. At each date $t \geq 1$ there are 'born' a constant number n of young people, each of whom is endowed with w_1 of a consumption good when young, and w_2 units when old. Subjects have *ex post* utility measured by

$$(1) \qquad\qquad \ln c_t^1 + \ln c_t^2,$$

and they can exchange consumption when young c_t^1 for consumption when old c_t^2 according to the budget constraints,

$$c_t^1 + m_t/p_t \leq w_1$$
$$c_t^2 \leq w_2 + m_t/p_{t+1},$$

where p_t is the price level at time t, and m_t is currency held from t to $t+1$.

A government issues an unbacked currency and uses it to finance a constant per-young-person deficit G. The government's budget constraint is

$$m_t - m_{t-1} = p_t G,$$

where here m_t is the supply of currency per young person. Each period, the price level is determined in a market in which the young trade some of their consumption goods to the old for currency.

Rational expectations solution

The fundamentals of this economy are not random. With perfect foresight about the price level, the saving function of the young is

$$(2) \qquad\qquad s_t = w_1 - c_t^1 = (w_1 - w_2 \pi_t)/2,$$

where $\pi_t = p_{t+1}/p_t$ is the gross rate of inflation. The government's budget constraint can be represented as

$$(3) \qquad h_t = h_{t-1}/\pi_{t-1} + G,$$

where $h_t = m_t/p_t$. The equilibrium condition is $h_t = s_t$. Equating s_t to h_t in (2) and (3) and eliminating h_t gives the autonomous difference equation in π_t:

$$(4) \qquad \pi_{t+1} = g(\pi_t),$$

where $g(\pi) = A_1 - A_2/\pi$, $A_1 = (w_1/w_2) - (2G/w_2) + 1$, $A_2 = w_1/w_2$.[2] The function g,which is graphed in Figure 1, determines the rational expectations dynamics of π_t.

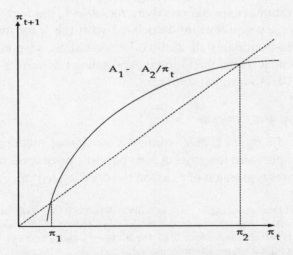

Figure 1. The equilibrium law of motion of the inflation rate. The curved line shows the equilibrium inflation rate in period $t+1$, π_{t+1}, as a function of the inflation rate in period t. The dotted line is the 45 degree line. The intersections of the curved line with the 45 degree line are stationary equilibrium inflation rates. An increase in G lowers the curve $A_1 - A_2/\pi_t$.

[2] See Sargent and Wallace (1982).

Figure 1 indicates that, if there exists an equilibrium, then there exist two stationary equilibria and a continuum of non-stationary equilibria. Evidently, of the two stationary equilibria, the one with the lower inflation rate is *unstable* under the rational expectations dynamics, while the one with the higher inflation rate is *stable*. The curve $A_1 - A_2/\pi_t$ shifts downward with an increase in G, because A_1 is decreasing in G. The comparative statics of the (unstable) *lower* stationary inflation rate are 'classical' in the sense that increases in G increase the stationary inflation rate. The comparative dynamics of the higher stationary inflation rate are anti-classical, a permanent increase in G causing the stationary inflation rate to fall because the economy is on the wrong side of a 'Laffer curve' in the inflation tax rate. Despite the fact that many classical doctrines in monetary theory depend on selecting the lower stationary equilibrium inflation rate, the rational expectations dynamics selects the higher one. The stationary equilibrium associated with the *lower* inflation rate Pareto-dominates all of the other equilibria, stationary or nonstationary. Thus, the rational expectations dynamics repels from the Pareto-optimal solution.[3]

The least squares dynamics

Marcet and Sargent (1989c) studied a version of this model in which people form forecasts of next period's price level using a least squares regression of price on the once lagged price.[4] The

---

[3] The strict Pareto ranking of these equilibria depends on the absence of heterogeneity within a generation in this model. In versions of the model with heterogeneity within generations (e.g., the borrowers and lenders of Wallace 1980), the equilibria are not Pareto-comparable.

[4] George Evans and Seppo Honkapohja (1992c) study the stability of 'sunspot equilibria' under adaptive least squares learning algorithms. In particular, they study the stability of sunspot equilibria that can be constructed near both stationary and periodic *fundamental* or non-sunspot equilibria. They show that the stability under adaptive learning of sunspot equilibria near fundamental equilibria is inherited from the stability under adaptive learning of the fundamental equilibria out of which they are constructed. For example, they show that the stability under learning of two-state sunspot equilibria that are constructed near

system with least squares learning has the same two stationary inflation rates as the system under rational expectations.
However, Marcet and Sargent showed how the least squares
dynamics *reverses* the stability of the two stationary equilibria:
under the least squares dynamics, the *lower* stationary inflation
rate is the limit of the dynamics for almost all starting values, if
any limiting value exists.[5] Bruno and Fischer (1990) discovered
similar outcomes in a closely related model in which they replaced perfect foresight with a version of Friedman's adaptive
expectations mechanism.

Marimon and Sunder's experiment

Marimon and Sunder (1992) designed an experimental environment to implement this economy.[6] They put a fixed number
of N participants in sessions of length T periods, unknown
to the participants, but chosen according to rules, known to
the subjects, that made the economy equivalent from participants' point of view to one that never ends. At each period
$1 \le t \le T$, $n < N/2$ of the subjects were designated as 'young,'
meaning that they were given an opportunity to submit a saving schedule telling the time t price level (or its reciprocal, the
value of money in terms of goods) at which they were willing to
supply time t output to the old for money in discrete amounts
$1, 2, 3, \ldots$. Marimon and Sunder linearly interpolated between
integers to get an individual's supply schedule, then summed
across the young to get total supply.[7] To determine the time t

period 2 fundamental equilibria requires stability under learning of the period
2 equilibrium; and that stability under learning of two-state sunspot equilibria
that are constructed out of *two* stationary (i.e. period 1) fundamental equilibria
requires stability under learning of *both* of the fundamental equilibria.

[5] See Bullard and Duffy (1993) for a warning not to overgeneralize from this
result.

[6] Marimon and Sunder show that equilibria outcomes of the overlapping-
generations economy are among the equilibria of the game that their experiment
defines.

[7] In forming their supply schedules, the subjects are implicitly forecasting the
price level at time $t + 1$, because their payoff depends on it.

price level, they set this supply schedule against a total demand schedule, composed of the sum of the demands for goods from the government and the old.

Subjects were randomly selected to be born or born again as young. Each period there were n young, n old, and $N - 2n$ agents temporarily sitting on the sidelines, awaiting rebirth. A participant was rewarded proportionately to his accumulated value of the criterion (1). In addition, those who sat on the sidelines participated in a 'forecasting game' from which they received additional rewards. At the beginning of each period, those on the sidelines were asked to forecast the market-clearing price for that period. The author of the forecast that came closest to the actual time t price was awarded a prize, and the winning forecast was announced to all subjects at the end of the period, together with the equilibrium time t price.

A session ended after forecasts for period $T + 1$ had been turned in, at which point Marimon and Sunder announced that the economy had ended at T. Marimon and Sunder then redeemed money holdings of the time T young at a price level equal to the average of the time $T + 1$ price that had been predicted by the sideliners. This procedure for ending the session was explained at the outset.

Experimental results

Figures 2 and 3 display some representative results, which are from Marimon and Sunder's Economy 7C, for which the parameters are $w_1 = 6, w_2 = 1, G = 1$. For this economy, stationary equilibrium net inflation rates are 100 and 200 percent, respectively. Figure 2 shows that the experimental results more closely approximate the least squares dynamics (indicated by the smooth dotted line converging to 100 percent from below) than the rational expectations dynamics (indicated by the smooth line converging to 200 percent from below). This pattern is indicative of all of Marimon and Sunder's results: the experimental dynamics on average are much better approximated by the adaptive dynamics than by the rational expectations dynamics.

For the same economy, Figure 3 plots the average forecast errors made by the sideliners in forecasting next period's price level, as well as the errors that would have been made by a least squares forecaster who used a regression of price on lagged price over the entire sample.[8] The forecast errors of the sideliners are comparable with the ones that would have been made by the least squares forecaster.

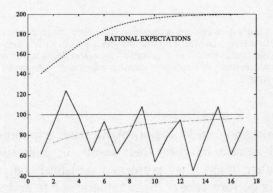

Figure 2. Path of inflation in Marimon and Sunder's 'Economy 7C' (solid line). Also shown are one path conforming to the rational expectations dynamics converging to the higher stationary inflation rate of 200 percent, and a dotted line converging from below to the lower stationary inflation rate of 100 percent, which depicts a path associated with Marcet and Sargent's least squares dynamics.

---

[8] These are 'honest' errors for the least squares forecaster, because the least squares regression coefficient used to make time t forecasts uses the observations on the experimental prices only through time $t - 1$.

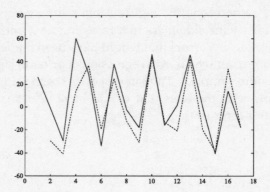

Figure 3. Solid line is record of sideliners' mean prediction errors in Marimon and Sunder's Economy 7C; dotted line is record of prediction error from least squares regressions of price on lagged price, using data up to time $t-1$.

Marimon and Sunder report many more experiments, and they analyze and interpret their results in interesting ways. Among other things, they perform a statistical analysis of the forecasting performance of the sideliners, and fit and test fixed-coefficient models of adaptive expectations *à la* Friedman and Cagan. This is part of an effort to learn about the details of the structure of adaptation that is propelling the experimental outcomes toward the low-inflation steady state. [9], [10]

[9] Can we expect laboratory experiments with paid students to increase our understanding of how actual monetary economies would operate? Even if the experimenter succeeds in inducing the preferences that he wants, the behavior of a randomly selected population of students might very well differ systematically from the self-selected and performance-censored sample of traders operating in foreign exchange markets. See Friedman and Sunder (1992) for an extensive analysis of experimental methods.

[10] If they were available, econometric studies of econometrically identifiable models with multiple equilibria would provide an alternative to using experi-

An example in the spirit of Brock

In the Marimon–Sunder setting, least squares adaptation and the experiments both seem to select the 'classical' stationary equilibrium, which happens to be Pareto-superior to the other stationary equilibrium. As a warning not always to expect adaptation to select a Pareto-superior outcome, I offer the following example, composed by taking a special version of William Brock's (1974) money-in-the-utility-function model of the demand for currency.[11]

An infinitely lived representative household maximizes

$$(5) \qquad \sum_{t=0}^{\infty} \beta^t (\ln c_t + \gamma \ln(m_t/p_t)), \quad \gamma > 0,$$

subject to the sequence of budget constraints,

$$c_t + m_t/p_t + b_t \leq m_{t-1}/p_t + R_{t-1}b_{t-1} + y,$$

and $m_{-1} > 0, b_{-1} = 0$ given. Here c_t is consumption of a single good, $y > 0$ is a fixed endowment of the consumption good, m_t

mental economies as a benchmark with which to compare the equilibria selected by adaptive algorithms. However, I know of few such econometric studies. One study is by Selahattin Imrohoroğlu (1993), who fits a rational expectations version of the same model used by Marimon and Sunder to data from the German hyperinflation. Imrohoroğlu estimates parameters that index the multiplicity of rational expectations equilibria. Despite the multiplicity of equilibria, his model is econometrically overidentified, which permits him to estimate which of the continuum of equilibria best describes the sample data, as measured by a Gaussian likelihood function. His estimates are consistent with the hypothesis that the observations come from an equilibrium with neither stochastic nor nonstochastic bubbles, but nevertheless are *not* consistent with the data having been generated from the low-inflation equilibrium. His estimated equilibrium is sliding along the bad side of the Laffer curve, toward the high stationary inflation rate. Thus, these results are inconsistent with the hypothesis that the data were generated from the equilibrium selected by the adaptive dynamics. Imrohoroğlu explains how this outcome emerges because the likelihood function is insisting on activating or 'mixing' *both* of the system's two endogenous roots (the low and high stationary nonstochastic equilibrium inflation rates) in order to match the salient lower frequency features of the data, namely, decreasing real balances and increasing inflation rates.

[11] This example was shown to me by Benjamin Bental.

is currency held from t to $t+1$, p_t is the time t price level, b_t is the amount lent at a gross real rate of interest of R_t. A government issues currency to finance a fixed level of expenditures $g > 0$, subject to the sequence of budget constraints $M_t - M_{t-1} = p_t g$, where M_t is the supply of currency, and where in equilibrium $M_t = m_t$.

Assume the restrictions on parameter values $\gamma(y - g) > g$. Then this model has a unique stationary equilibrium, with $R = 1/\beta$, gross inflation rate $\pi = p_{t+1}/p_t$ determined by the value of π that solves $g = \gamma(y - g)(1 - \pi^{-1})/(1 - \beta/\pi)$.[12] This stationary equilibrium value of π has the 'classical' property that it is increasing in the value of the government deficit g.

However, the model also has a continuum of nonstationary equilibria, indexed by initial price levels that are lower than the initial price level associated with the stationary equilibrium. In all of these equilibria, $\lim_{t \to \infty} \pi_t = \beta$, so that these equilibria are characterized by *deflation*. These equilibria exist because the demand for currency induced by the preference ordering (5) is so elastic with respect to the rate of return on currency that there is room for a system of expectations in which the government can collect enough seigniorage to finance g even while it pays out interest on its currency through deflation. These equilibria are definitely not 'classical,' because they imply that, within limits, higher values of g are not associated with higher permanent values of inflation. An example of a nonstationary equilibrium is shown in Figure 4, which starts from an initial rate of return on currency of unity. For this example, we set $\gamma = 1, \beta = 1/1.05, y = 11, g = 1$. Notice how the rate of return on currency approaches $1/\beta = 1.05$, and how the equilibrium level of real balances explodes.

This model shares with the overlapping-generations model

---

[12] Namely,

$$\pi = \frac{(y - g)\gamma - \beta g}{(y - g)\gamma - g}.$$

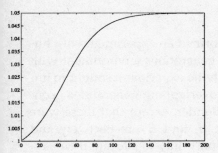

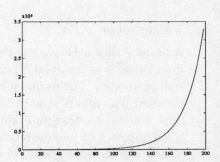

Figure 4a. Time series of gross rate of return on currency (reciprocal of gross inflation rate) in Brock economy with $c = 10, g = 1, \beta = 1/1.05, \gamma = 1$, under rational expectations dynamics.

Figure 4b. Time series of real value of currency in Brock economy under rational expectations dynamics.

the property that the 'classical' stationary equilibrium is *unstable* under the rational expectations dynamics. However, unlike the overlapping-generations model studied by Marimon and Sunder, the non-stationary rational expectations equilibria all Pareto-dominate the 'classical' stationary equilibrium.

What about the behavior of this model under 'adaptive' dynamics? If we were to use a version of the least squares learning mechanism studied by Marcet and Sargent (1989c), we would find that the 'classical' equilibrium is stable, while the non-stationary equilibria are not. Thus, this example shares with the overlapping-generations example the property that least squares dynamics selects a 'classical' stationary equilibrium. But the example also serves to warn us not to expect as a general rule that least squares dynamics will select a Pareto-superior equilibrium.[13]

[13] See Moore (1993) for an application of least squares learning to select between stationary rational expectations equilibria in a model of Howitt and McAfee

Exchange rate experiments

The experiment

Jasmina Arifovic (1993) has performed an experiment with human subjects in an overlapping-generations environment with two currencies. The model which the experiment sought to implement was identical with the overlapping-generations economy studied by Marimon and Sunder, except that there were fixed supplies of two currencies, H_1 and H_2, respectively, and young agents were given the opportunity to allocate their savings between the two currencies. Arifovic set the experiment up a little differently from Marimon and Sunder's. She asked each young person to choose both a savings rate and a fraction allocating total savings between the two currencies. Let the savings rate for person i be s_i and the portion of the savings going to currency 1 be λ_i. Then the price levels at time t were determined as described in Chapter 4, namely by

$$p_{1t} = \frac{H_1}{\sum \lambda_{it} s_{it}}, \quad p_{2t} = \frac{H_2}{\sum (1 - \lambda_{it}) s_{it}}.$$

Also, Arifovic split the group of N participants into two groups of equal size, one of which was young in odd periods, the other being young in even periods. Thus, unlike the situation in the Marimon–Sunder experiments, participants knew in advance when they would be born again. Arifovic also ended the experiments differently from Marimon and Sunder. In the final period, which was unknown beforehand to the participants, after the young people made their saving and portfolio decisions, she told the participants that this was the last period. It was known in advance that she would redeem money held by this last generation of young at a price level determined as the average of the price levels of the previous two periods.

(1988). Moore finds that the low-employment equilibria is not stable under least squares learning but that the high employment equilibrium can be.

Exchange rate paths

Figures 5a, 5b, and 5c display exchange rate paths from three sessions of Arifovic's experiments. The same set of subjects was used for each of the three sessions.[14] Figure 5d displays the total saving rates of the young in experiment 1. For purposes of comparison, one can compute that in the rational expectations equilibrium the savings rate should be $(w_1 - w_2)/2 = 5$.

The exchange rate fluctuates within a range from 0.5 to 2. It does not settle down to a constant; if anything, the amplitude of the fluctuations grows between sessions 2 and 3. Figures 5d and 5e display the savings rates for session 3.

Evidently, the simple least squares adaptive model used in Chapter 4 does a poor job of explaining these experimental data. But using a version of a genetic algorithm,[15] Arifovic has produced an economy with a population of adaptive agents that is capable of generating much exchange rate volatility. We now turn to her model.

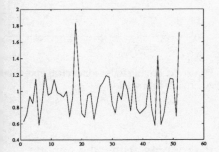

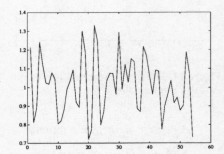

Figure 5a. Exchange rates from Arifovic's first session.

Figure 5b. Exchange rates from Arifovic's second session.

[14] Parameter values were $w_1 = 11, w_2 = 1, H_1 = 10, H_2 = 10$.

[15] Arifovic added what she called an *election* operator to the sequence of operators used by Holland to define the genetic algorithm. The election operator tests the 'children' of a pair of parents to see whether they are fitter as judged by last period's data fed into the performance criterion. If the children are fitter by that measure, they replace their parents. Otherwise, the parents live on and the children are not born.

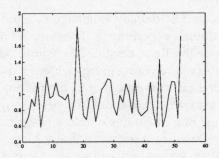

Figure 5c. Exchange rates from Arifovic's third session.

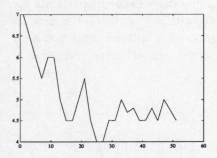

Figure 5d. Saving Rates for odd agents from Arifovic's first session.

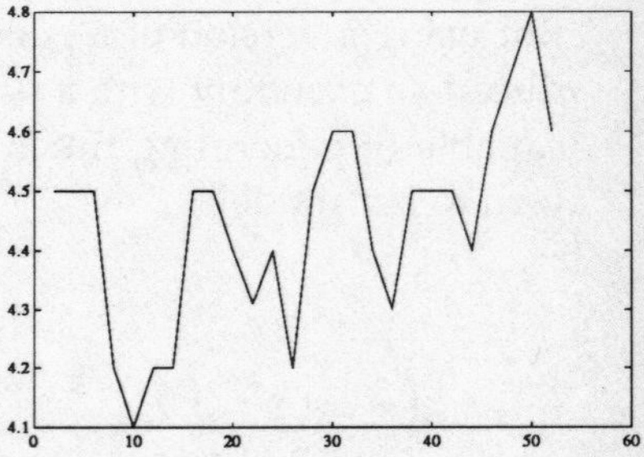

Figure 5e. Saving Rates for even agents from Arifovic's first session.

A genetic algorithm economy

Arifovic studied a version of this economy using the genetic algorithm. The economy was inhabited by overlapping generations of two *populations* of agents of fixed sizes $N = 30$. A population of N young agents consisted of a list of N binary strings of length $\ell = 30$. The first 20 elements of a string were used to encode the saving decision parameter s_i, and the second 10 were used to encode the portfolio division fraction λ_i. The 'fitness' of strings was evaluated according to the *ex post* value of the utility function (1), evaluated after the lifetime experience of the agent had been realized.[16]

Figure 6 shows parts of a record of exchange rates from the genetic economy.[17] The realized exchange rates are more variable than those found in Arifovic's experiments. There are some quiescent periods for the exchange rate, as shown in parts of Figure 6d, which covers observations 1801 through 1900, but they come to an end.

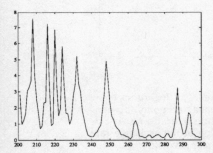

Figure 6a. Exchange rate from genetic economy (observations 201–300).

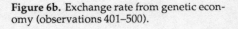

Figure 6b. Exchange rate from genetic economy (observations 401–500).

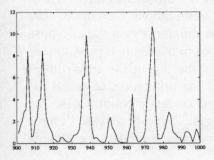

Figure 6c. Exchange rate from genetic economy (observations 901–1000).

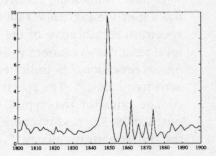

Figure 6d. Exchange rate from genetic economy (observations 1801–1900).

[16] Arifovic carried along two populations of odd and even agents, letting each population choose every other period, for the reasons explained in the Chapter 4 discussion of the least squares adaptive exchange rate model.
[17] Arifovic generated 20,000 observations, and we show pieces of the first 2000.

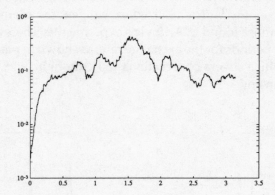

Figure 7. Spectrum of difference of logarithm of exchange rate for Arifovic's genetic economy (observations 1000–2000). The spectrum indicates nearly random walk behavior for the log of the exchange rate, modified by the presence of mean reversion.

Figure 7 shows the spectrum of a windsorized difference of the log of the exchange rate for observations 1000–2000. The spectrum is indicative of the first difference of a series whose level resembles a random walk, except that there is pronounced 'mean reversion,' as indicated by the dip in the spectrum at zero frequency.[18] The spectra of log differences of actual exchange rates for two typical hard currency countries for the postwar 1973 period resemble Figure 7, except they don't have the dip at zero frequency.[19] *Vis à vis* the model of exchange

---

[18] 'Windsorizing' is achieved by naming two bounds (B_1, B_2) with $B_1 < B_2$, and replacing every observation *less* than B_1 with B_1 and every observation *greater* than B_2 with B_2. Where data are suspected of having distributions with infinite variances, windsorizing is a technique devised to assure that spectral densities are well-defined.

[19] The economic environment in which Arifovic's genetic algorithms operate does not contain any of the classic forces for low-frequency divergences in

rates with Newton–Raphson adapting agents, Arifovic's genetic model generates much more 'realistic' exchange rate behavior.

exchange rates, such as persistently different monetary and deficit policies.

7
Applications

I conclude this essay by pointing to some promising applications of the methods that we have surveyed, and also to some limitations.

Evolutionary programming

We have studied several examples in which systems of adaptive agents eventually find their way to a rational expectations equilibrium, and we know from results in the literature that there is a big class of other models where convergence will also occur. The examples in this book have all been ones that are simple enough for us to compute equilibria beforehand, then watch how fast and to which equilibrium the adaptive system converged. The idea of *evolutionary programming* is to use the equilibrium-finding tendency of collections of adapting agents to *compute* equilibria for us.[1]

Kiyotaki–Wright search models

Adaptive methods have been used to discover equilibria of enriched versions of Kiyotaki and Wright's (1989) search model of monies. Kiyotaki and Wright's original model is an infinitely repeated 'Wicksell triangle' economy. There are continua[2] of three types of household. Each type of household produces its own type of good, but likes to consume only the good of the type of consumer to its 'right' along the triangle. Goods are

---

[1] We have already seen that Marcet's method of parameterized expectations has many aspects of a learning or adaptation algorithm.

[2] The continua are of equal measure.

indivisible, and each consumer can store only one unit of any good at a time, with costs of storage differing among goods. Each period, a consumer is pairwise randomly matched with one of the other consumers whom he/she expects never to meet again. Kiyotaki and Wright's economy is set up to preclude coincidence of wants, and to require that trade be mediated via a 'medium of exchange,' a good that some of the traders occasionally take and hold in the expectation that they can trade it later for the good that they want to consume. Kiyotaki and Wright formulate Nash equilibria of this economy, and describe a method for stationary equilibria. A stationary equilibrium for Kiyotaki and Wright's model is a collection of trading strategies for each type, and a set of probabilities of meetings between households storing different types of goods.

Marimon, McGrattan, and Sargent (1990) put collections of Holland classifier systems inside two of Kiyotaki and Wright's economic environments[3] and watched them converge to an equilibrium. Litterman and Knez (1989) put three populations determined by a genetic algorithm into a Kiyotaki–Wright environment, and these also found their way to an equilibrium. Encouraged by these results, Marimon, McGrattan, and Sargent created a *pentagonal* version of Kiyotaki and Wright's environment, with five types of households and goods, and populated it with five types of classifier systems. This system settled down to a collection of trading strategies and probabilities that could then be verified to be an equilibrium.

The idea of evolutionary programming is to use adaptive algorithms to inspire a 'guess,' then to use the 'guess and verify' method of solving the functional equations that determine an equilibrium. Randall Wright (1993) has used this method to compute the equilibrium of a version of the original Kiyotaki–Wright model in which the fractions of different types of agents

---

[3] Kiyotaki and Wright described two environments, model A and model B, that differed in the arrangement of preferences for goods within the Wicksell triangle.

are endogenous.[4] Instead of having equal measures of the three types of households, he let there be fractions θ_j that are chosen to make the payoffs to the three types of agents $j = 1, 2, 3$ equal. He set up an evolutionary system to find such an equilibrium, whose equilibrium conditions are all of the equilibrium conditions of the original Kiyotaki–Wright model, plus the restriction that payoffs are equal across types. For fixed vector θ, Wright used the methods of Kiyotaki and Wright to compute a 'fixed-θ' equilibrium, then calculated payoffs to the different types. Then he let the fraction of the types evolve, according to a version of the 'reproduction operator' within the genetic algorithm. The share vector θ eventually evolved to a point at which payoffs were equalized. Such a point is automatically an equilibrium, because by construction it builds in all of the equilibrium conditions.[5]

Wright used evolutionary methods not because he was interested in the evolutionary dynamics, but as a method of finding an equilibrium. From this standpoint, it is interesting how Wright divided the work of equilibrium computation between himself and the adaptive agents. For each θ vector along the evolutionary process, Wright computed a fixed-θ equilibrium, and computed the expected value of the infinite-horizon payoff function for all agents at that equilibrium. He then 'told' the evolutionary process those theoretical payoffs, and let the fraction of agents adapt to them. Notice how this division of labor makes the process hard to interpret in terms of 'real-time dynamics' because Wright is giving agents information about payoffs that they could acquire only by experiencing very long histories within fixed-θ regimes. But from the viewpoint of Wright's interest in equilibrium computation, the process's lack

---

[4] Wright used this model to capture some responses that are shut down by Kiyotaki and Wright's assumption of fixed and equal shares, which affects the payoffs to types in ways that provoke no response in the original model.

[5] Matsuyama, Kiyotaki, and Matsui (1992) used evolutionary methods to determine the stability of equilibria of an extension of the Kiyotaki–Wright model in which multiple currencies can emerge.

of credibility as real-time dynamics is irrelevant.

How adaptive agents teach smart economists

In using systems of adaptive agents to generate a 'guess,' we are counting on the tendency of these systems of adaptive agents, as plodding as they are, eventually to find their ways to equilibria that we economists (who, after all, made up the environment!) have difficulty finding, despite all of our advantages relative to those agents in terms of knowledge about the way the whole system is put together.

There is nothing magic or new going on here. The adaptive agents are 'teaching' the economist in the same sense that any numerical algorithm for solving nonlinear equations 'teaches' a mathematician. When these agents can 'teach' us something, it is because we designed them to do so.

Solving recurrent single-agent problems

There exist a number of examples in which an artificial device has been trained to learn a good strategy to apply within an environment that is complicated enough to challenge an expert in decision theory. The method is simple: put the artificial device within a computer representation of the environment, and use simulations to train it.

An iterated prisoner's dilemma

Robert Axelrod (1987) used the genetic algorithm to train a population to play against the computer programs that had been submitted by participants in his round-robin computer tournament to play the iterated prisoners' dilemma. He encoded strategies as binary strings of length 70, with the last 64 of the bits used to dictate play following *each* of the 64 possible histories of play in the history of the *three* previous moves,[6] and

---

[6] There are four possible combinations of moves each time the one-period game is played, meaning that there are 4^3 possible histories of length 3.

the first six bits being used to encode initial play. The algorithm produced a strategy that would have won the tournament, and in particular would have outplayed the 'tit-for-tat' strategy that won the tournament.[7] Interestingly enough, the winning genetic strategy behaved much like 'tit-for-tat' when confronted with non-tit-for-tat strategies, but sufficiently tougher against tit-for-tat that it could take advantage of it.

A double oral auction

Rust, Palmer, and Miller (1992) set up a computer tournament to play the double oral auction. Participants submitted programs encoding their strategies, then the computer ran auctions, and kept accounts of earnings. Participants received monetary rewards in proportion to those earnings.

The winning strategy in the tournament was submitted by a graduate student at the University of Minnesota, Todd Kaplan. Kaplan's strategy abstains from making bids or offers, but waits and watches other people make bids and offers, then 'steals the trade' when bids and offers get close enough together. A market composed mostly of traders like Kaplan would have behaved badly, and not to Kaplan's benefit, but enough other participants submitted strategies with aggressive bid and offer components that Kaplan prospered.

Rust, Palmer, and Miller (1992) went on to use neural networks to encode a class of potential strategies, then to train them by allowing them to compete against each other and a collection of other strategies for very long simulations. In choosing a class of neural nets, Rust, Palmer, and Miller were in effect choosing the domain of a nonlinear function (i.e., what information the strategy could potentially condition on) and the class of nonlinear decision rules that could potentially be learned (controlled by the number of 'hidden units'). Rust, Palmer and

---

[7] The genetic algorithm had a big advantage over the participants in the tournament because it got to practice against them, while they could only guess what opponents' strategies would be.

Miller used a genetic algorithm to estimate or train the neural nets. There were neural nets for both 'buyers' and 'sellers.'

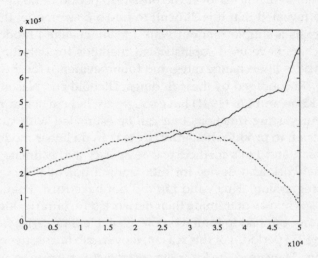

Figure 1. Evolution of capital for two 'sellers' in computer tournament of double oral auction. The solid line is the cumulated earnings of a 'Kaplan' seller; the dotted line is the cumulated earnings of what for a long time seemed to be the best neural network seller.

During the early part of one of Rust, Palmer, and Miller's simulations with 52 sellers and buyers, with some of them being neural net traders, one of the neural networks sellers does better than a Kaplan seller. Figure 1 records the cumulative earnings for the best neural network seller and Kaplan. The superiority of the neural network over Kaplan eventually vanishes later in the simulation. Thus, after a very long training session, Rust, Palmer, and Miller failed to produce a neural network that would have done better than Kaplan's. These results show the difficulty confronted by a relatively unprompted artificial device in discovering rules that defeat the simple but shrewd strategy devised by the human Kaplan.[8]

---

[8] Rust, Palmer, and Miller (1992) make interesting observations on the extent

Forecasting the exchange rate

Estimates of vector autoregressions for exchange rates for leading 'hard currencies' over the post-1973 period of floating rates
have revealed that it is difficult to find a *linear* model that out-
forecasts a simple random walk (or 'no change') model. Researchers have used sophisticated methods for detecting nonlinearities in exchange rates, and found evidence for their presence. Encouraged by these findings, Diebold and Nason (1990)
and Kuan and Liu (1991) have sought to find particular nonlinear forecasting functions that can be estimated with sufficient
precision to produce better forecasts than do linear models.[9]

Kuan and Liu's method was to specify and estimate a neural network as a device for estimating a potentially nonlinear
autoregression. Kuan and Liu did not have Rust, Palmer, and
Miller's luxury of training their network on arbitrarily long simulations, but had to train it on the available time series from the
post-1973 period. For this reason, they had to face issues of overfitting. They used the Rissanen complexity criterion to arrive at
models for a collection of exchange rates, which they then used
to produce and evaluate 'honest forecasts.'

Let S_t be the exchange rate, and $y_t = \log S_t - \log S_{t-1}$.
The simplest model that Kuan and Lin fitted was of the form
$y_{t+1} = f(y_t) + \eta_{t+1}$, where η_{t+1} is a forecasting error, and $f(y)$ is
determined by a neural network of the form

$$f(y) = \beta_0 + \sum_{j=1}^{6} \beta_j S(\gamma_{0j} + \gamma_{1j} y),$$

where $S(\cdot)$ is the sigmoid function $S(z) = 1/(1+\exp(-z))$. Kuan
and Liu fitted their models to daily closing prices from 1987 to

to which simulations of markets populated by groups of neural networks look
like those populated by human players of the double oral auction.

[9] Diebold and Nason (1990) used nonparametric methods to see if nonlinearities that have been detected in post-Bretton Woods exchange rates could be
exploited to generate better point predictions than are yielded by a linear model.
They did not find them.

1991 for five countries, then used the models to forecast out of
sample. Figure 2 shows the nonlinear function estimated by
Kuan and Liu for the yen–dollar exchange rate.[10] We use two
scales, to supply a magnifying glass for spotting the nonlinearity
that the procedure has detected. The figures show how the neural network has managed to detect only a minuscule departure
from the 'martingale' model ($f(y) = 0$), and how in this case the
autoregression is linear to a very good approximation.

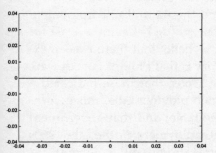 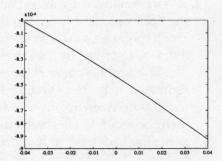

Figure 2a. Estimated neural net function $f(\cdot)$
for mapping change in log of yen-dollar exchange rate today into prediction for change
in log of yen-dollar exchange rate tomor-
row. The neural net essentially estimates
a 'martingale difference' model for the log
exchange rate.

Figure 2b. Estimated neural net for forecasting yen-dollar exchange rate finer scale on
coordinate axis. Notice the very mild nonlinearity.

It is interesting that these techniques fail to find substantial
deviations from linearity that would be useful for predicting

[10] Kuan and Lin used two types of estimators. The first was an 'on-line' algorithm of the kind described in Chapter 4. The second was an 'off-line' version
of nonlinear least squares. I report the results for nonlinear least squares. Kuan
and Liu discuss how the 'on-line' algorithm can be used to make several passes
through the data, with the final estimates from the last pass being used as the
initial estimates from the next pass.

in this particular context.[11] Undoubtedly, application of such techniques in other contexts will detect deviations from linearity that are exploitable for forecasting.[12]

A model of policy-makers' learning

Within the rational expectations literature in macroeconomics, there is a strand that interprets the post-World War II covariation of unemployment and inflation in the United States as reflecting the interaction between a private sector whose behavior was summarized by an expectational Phillips curve embodying both rational expectations and the natural unemployment rate hypothesis, and a government whose behavior at least for a time was driven by the erroneous belief that there was an exploitable Phillips curve.[13] The story is that Phillips curves were estimated with data through the 1960s; that these indicated a tradeoff between inflation and unemployment that the government believed to have been exploitable; and that government policy-makers tried to lower unemployment in the late 1960s and early 1970s by managing aggregate demand to generate inflation. The story asserts that the consequence of these actions was to cause the Phillips curve to shift up adversely, leading to higher inflation with no benefits in terms of lower unemployment on average.

However, this story has been disputed by various fitters of 1960s style Phillips curves, who argued that their econometric procedures were adaptive, and were able to detect the adverse shift in the Phillips curve swiftly enough to give sound policy advice.

---

[11] Canova (1993) uses a Bayesian vector autoregression with time-varying coefficients to represent and estimate a model of exchange rates with particular types of nonlinearities. See his paper for a discussion of the types of nonlinearities that seem to infest exchange rate data.

[12] Kuan and Liu also fitted what amount to higher-order nonlinear univariate autoregressive models for exchange rate log differences.

[13] For a discussion of some of the issues, see Lucas (1981, pp. 221, 283).

Christopher Sims (1988) described an econometric specification capable of representing both the 'natural rate' story, with its combination of a rational private sector and an irrational government, and the alternative story that traditional Phillips curve fitters caught on to what was happening soon enough to give the government timely advice. Sims wanted a manageable model that could formalize the informal procedures that Phillips curve fitters in practice used to protect themselves against some of the effects of specification errors. He formulated a model of boundedly rational macroeconomic policy-makers who use a plausible econometric strategy for learning about a Phillips curve tradeoff. The model can have multiple types of equilibria, one of which displays the feature that introducing uncertainty into the government's (erroneous) model can sometimes lead the system toward an approximately optimal outcome. Heetaik Chung (1990) estimated a version of the model for post-World War II time series from the United States. This is the only econometrically serious macroeconomic implementation of bounded rationality of which I know.

The model is an extended version of Kydland and Prescott's (1977) Phillips curve example. The rate of inflation is decomposed as

$$(1) \qquad \pi_t = g_{t-1} + \eta_t,$$

where π_t is the rate of inflation at time t, g_{t-1} is the *expected* rate of inflation as of time $t - 1$ (i.e., $E\pi_t|I_{t-1} = g_{t-1}$, where I_{t-1} is the public's time $t - 1$ information), and η_t is the public's error in forecasting inflation. The government can control g_{t-1} but not the forecast error η_t, which is assumed to be orthogonal to information available to the public at dates earlier than t. Unknown to the government, there is truly a natural-rate Phillips curve of the form

$$(2) \qquad U_t = U^* - \theta(\pi_t - g_{t-1}) + u_t,$$

where $\theta > 0$, U^* is the natural rate of unemployment, and $\{u_t\}$

is a covariance stationary stochastic process that is orthogonal to $(\pi_t - g_{t-1})$. Only the *unexpected* part of inflation influences the unemployment rate, but the government does not (at least in the beginning) realize this.

At time t, policy-makers (incorrectly) estimate that the Phillips curve is of the (non-expectational) form

$$(3) \qquad U_t = \hat{\alpha}_{0t} + \hat{\alpha}_{1t}\pi_t + \epsilon_t,$$

where $(\hat{\alpha}_{0t}, \hat{\alpha}_{1t})$ are the government's time t estimates of parameters of the Phillips curve, and ϵ_t is a statistical residual, which the government believes to be serially uncorrelated. The policy-maker sets g_{t-1} myopically to maximize

$$(4) \qquad -0.5E(U_t^2 + \pi_t^2),$$

subject to the perceived constraints

$$(5) \qquad \begin{aligned} \pi_t &= g_{t-1} + \eta_t \\ U_t &= \hat{\alpha}_{0t} + \hat{\alpha}_{1t}\pi_t + \epsilon_t. \end{aligned}$$

Therefore, the government's decision rule is

$$(6) \qquad g_{t-1} = -\hat{\alpha}_{0t}\hat{\alpha}_{1t}/(1 + \hat{\alpha}_{1t}^2).$$

Constant coefficient beliefs

As a benchmark, Sims and Chung first formalize a least squares learning process that in the limit converges to Kydland and Prescott's 'consistent equilibrium.' The government believes a version of model (3) in which (apart from estimation error) the coefficients α_0, α_1 are constant over time. Each period the government updates its estimates using ordinary least squares, and then implements (6) using its latest parameter estimates. This practice generates a 'self-referential' system because the actual relation between inflation and unemployment depends on the government's false perception of the relation (3) and the action (6) that it takes on the basis of that perception. This produces a least-squares learning process that converges to Kydland and Prescott's consistent equilibrium in which the coefficient estimates eventually satisfy

(7)
$$\alpha_0 = (1 + \theta^2)U^*$$
$$\alpha_1 = -\theta.$$

Consequently, g_{t-1} converges to θU^*, with $U_t \doteq U^* - \theta \eta_t + u_t$. This outcome gives lower utility to the government than it could have attained if it had understood that the true Phillips curve was (2). If the government had known the true Phillips curve, it would have attained the same unemployment rate it eventually got, but with $g_{t-1} = 0$, which evidently would have been better. This outcome comes from Kydland and Prescott's 'optimal policy.'

Random coefficient beliefs

Sims and Chung modified the model in a way designed to attribute model uncertainty to the government. They assumed that the government's beliefs are described by a random-coefficients version of model (3) in which the government suspects that the 'true coefficients' are taking a random walk:

(8)
$$\begin{bmatrix} \alpha_{0t} \\ \alpha_{1t} \end{bmatrix} = \begin{bmatrix} \alpha_{0t-1} \\ \alpha_{1t-1} \end{bmatrix} + \begin{bmatrix} \nu_{1t} \\ \nu_{2t} \end{bmatrix},$$

where ν_t is a (2×1) Gaussian white noise with $E\nu_t = 0$ and $E\nu_t\nu_t' = \sigma_\nu$ being diagonal with $E\nu_{it}^2 = \sigma_{\nu_i}^2$. The parameters in σ_ν index the government's degree of confidence in the constant-coefficient, linear specification.

Sims and Chung assumed that the government applies the Kalman filter to estimate the random coefficients model comprised by (3) and (8), given values of the parameters σ_ν; and that the government continues to make policy on the basis of the myopic rule (6).[14] Sims showed how this model can exhibit two types of behavior. First, some histories of the model look like (noisy) versions of the model in which the government has constant-coefficient beliefs, and converge to the vicinity of a consistent equilibrium. However, other histories converge to a stochastic process that spends most of its time near the *optimal* zero-inflation outcome. Along these paths, because of its willingness to entertain random coefficients in the model it is fitting, the government is rather quickly learning (without putting the economy through a big inflation) that the Phillips curve tradeoff is poor, which dampens its enthusiasm for exploiting it. Which type of path emerges depends partly on the parameter values (especially the parameters σ_ν indexing the government's certainty about the form of the model). Notice how these two types of paths represent formalizations of the story and the counter-story described at the beginning of this section.

Econometric implementation

Chung specified and estimated an enlarged version of this model using post-war US time series. He extended the specifications of the true and government-perceived Phillips curve (2) and (3), respectively, to permit lag structures more capable of matching the data, partly by explicitly modelling serial correlation structures of disturbance processes. As the econometrically free parameters he took $(\theta, U^*, \sigma_\nu, \hat{\alpha}(0))$ and the variances of the other shocks in the model, where $\hat{\alpha}(0)$ is the prior mean of the α vector, used to initiate the government's Kalman filter. He wrote down a Gaussian quasi-likelihood function conditioned on a data record $\{U_t, \pi_t\}_{t=1}^{T}$, and maximized it with respect to the free parameters. This procedure permitted Chung to estimate a model of the government's learning process. A product of Chung's estimation is a history of the government's beliefs

[14] The Kalman filter can be formulated as a stochastic approximation algorithm. For example, see Ljung, Pflug, and Walk (1992, pp. 99–100).

$\{\hat{\alpha}_{it}\}$ and its decision rules (6).

Thus, Chung estimated and discussed the altered state of the government's perceptions about the Phillips curve, and a time-varying decision rule of a form extending (6) during the post-war period, and advanced intriguing interpretations about how his estimates match up with informal non-econometric interpretations of how beliefs about the Phillips curve impinged on government macroeconomic decision-making.

In addition to its interesting substance, the work of Chung and Sims is important for demonstrating the practical possibility of econometrically implementing a model in which the econometrician is imputing the application of non-trivial econometrics procedures to one or more of the agents within the estimated model. If bounded rationality is to be put to work in macroeconomics, this is only the first of this type of work that we shall see.

Limitations

Prompting

Rational expectations imposes a specific kind of consistency condition on an economic model. The idea of bounded rationality is perhaps best defined by what it is *not* (rational expectations), a definition that captures the malleability of bounded rationality as a principle of model building. Even after we have adopted a particular class of algorithms to represent the adaptive behavior of a collection of agents, we have seen repeatedly that we face innumerable decisions about how to represent decision-making processes and the ways that they are updated.

As model builders, we decide how much agents know in advance, what they don't know and must learn about, and the particular methods they have to use to learn.[15] Do they know their utility and profit functions, or must they learn about them?

---

[15] We decide how they are 'hard-wired.'

Do they know calculus and dynamic programming, or must they only use 'trial and error' methods? Do they learn only from their own past experiences or from those of others?[16] To what class of approximating functions do we restrict them in specifying what they learn about?

Contributions to the bounded rationality literature have taken many different stands on these issues. The example of Bray in Chapter 5, and some of the examples described by Marcet and Sargent (1989a, 1989b), give the artificial agents a lot of 'prompting.' In Bray's model, agents know the correct supply curve, and must only estimate the correct conditional expectation to plug into it.[17] Some of Marcet and Sargent's examples are in the adaptive control tradition of assuming that agents use dynamic programming to compute an optimal decision rule, that they know the parameters of their return function and the parametric *form* of the transition function, but that they lack knowledge of the parameters of the transition function. So each period, these agents are supposed to use Litterman–Sims-style econometric methods to update an estimated vector autoregressive representation of the unknown pieces of their transition equation, then to solve their dynamic programming problem given their most recent estimates of the transition law.[18]

The classifier systems that live in Marimon, McGrattan, and Sargent's (1990) version of Kiyotaki–Wright models receive much less prompting than the agents of Bray and Marcet and Sargent, but they still get a lot. Marimon, McGrattan, and Sargent's agents are not told their utility functions; they recognize utility only when they experience it. They are ignorant of dynamic programming, and can come to appreciate the consequences of

[16] Ellison and Fudenberg (1992) study evolutionary systems in which people condition their choices on how a fraction of agents in the population have acted in the past.

[17] In games of fictitious play, players play best responses to estimates of probability distributions formed from histograms of past play. Though the setting is different, the spirit is the same as Bray's.

[18] This scheme is irrational because agents are ignoring the consequences of estimation uncertainty when solving their dynamic programming problem.

sequences of actions only by trying them out, then experiencing the utility of their consequences. Still, they are prompted. They are told when to choose and what information to use. The size and structure of their classifier systems, including the details of the accounting system, and the generalization and specialization operators, are chosen for them by Marimon, McGrattan, and Sargent, who obviously had an eye on specifying these things so that the artificial agents would have a good chance to learn to play the Kiyotaki–Wright equilibrium.[19]

Simplicity

All of the examples that we have studied are very simple in terms of the econometric problems with which we have confronted our artificial agents. We have given our agents the task of learning either a time-invariant decision rule or a collection of conditional expectations. It is easy to imagine settings in which more complicated tasks would be assigned to the agents. Useful ways of complicating these tasks can be found by following the topics treated in a modern econometrics course. For example, we might make our agents learn about the parameters of an econometric *structure* using the methods of classical simultaneous equations or rational expectations econometrics. The point of these methods is not to learn about a single decision rule or probability distribution but about a mapping from parameters characterizing policy regimes to functions or probability distributions.[20]

Bounded rationality and the econometricians

Bounded rationality is a movement to make model agents behave more like econometricians. Despite the compliment thereby paid to their kind, macroeconometricians have shown very little interest in applying models of bounded rationality to data.

[19] See Marimon and McGrattan (1993) for a critical review of adaptive algorithms within the context of games. Also see Kreps (1990).
[20] See Hurwicz (1946) for a brief discussion.

Within the economics profession, the impulse to build models populated by econometricians has come primarily from theorists with different things on their minds from most econometricians.

Applied time series econometricians have largely ignored the bounded rationality program because they accept a canon embodied in Lucas's warning to 'beware of theorists bearing free parameters.'[21] Within a specific economic model, an econometric consequence of replacing rational agents with boundedly rational ones is to add a number of parameters describing their beliefs and the motion of their beliefs.[22] For example, relative to a rational expectations model, count the number of additional free parameters that would be associated with implementing the model of Bray that appeared in Chapter 5. For a single-agent version of the model, one would add the parameter β_0 characterizing initial beliefs, and a parameter γ_0 initiating the gain sequence. One might want to add other parameters characterizing the shape of the $\{\gamma_t\}$ sequence. These parameters would be a nuisance to estimate for technical reasons associated with the fact that, because of Bray's result about convergence to rational expectations, these parameters only influence transient dynamics: the asymptotic distribution of $\{p_t\}$ contains no information about these parameters. Multiple-agent versions of Bray's model would have additional parameters, and so would any of the larger example models that we have studied.

Transition dynamics

Because of the preceding limitations, the literature on adaptive decision processes seems to me to fall far short of providing a secure foundation for a good theory of real-time transition dynamics. There are problems of arbitrariness and the need for

[21] John Taylor (1975) and Christopher Sims (1988) have used systems with adaptive agents to make interesting theoretical points. We have described how Chung (1990) implemented such a model empirically.

[22] The model of Chung (1990) described above illustrates these points in a simple context, while also demonstrating that such an analysis is feasible.

prompting, with a concommitant sensitivity of outcomes to details of adaptive algorithms. There is the extreme simplicity of the learning tasks typically assigned in the models compared even with the econometric learning tasks assigned in econometric classes, to say nothing of those implicitly being resolved by firms and households. In particular, the environments into which we have cast our adaptive agents seem much more stable and hospitable than the real-life situations for which we would want transition dynamics. On the purely technical side, there is the shortage of results on rates of convergence, and the need severely to restrict the distribution of agents' beliefs in order to get tractable models. And most important, and surely partly a consequence of the earlier limitations, applied econometricians have supplied us with almost no evidence about how adaptive models might work empirically.

It would not be wise or fair to end this essay by dwelling on the failure of adaptive methods so far to have 'hit a home run' by giving us a good theory of transition dynamics. The problem of transition dynamics is difficult and long-standing. So maybe it should count as a single, or at least a sacrifice fly, that these methods have sharpened our appreciation of the problem. And adaptive methods have given us other hits.

Successes and promises

I finish this essay by listing the things about adaptive algorithms in macroeconomics that I think will become more and more useful. Despite my reservations about them as theories of real-time dynamics, I like adaptive algorithms as devices for selecting equilibria.[23] Evolutionary programming is a valuable tool for computing equilibria, and is likely to be applied often. Econometricians are likely to continue to find useful devices in

---

[23] I know that it is inconsistent to doubt the real-time dynamics but keep the equilibria selected by them. I confess that my affection for the selection performed in the monetary models described in Chapter 6 is partly driven by my prior conviction that the selected equilibria seem sensible to me.

the literatures on adaptation. Econometricians are now using genetic algorithms and stochastic Gauss–Newton procedures, even if the agents in the models that they are estimating are not.

References

Aarts, Emile and Korst, Jan (1990), *Simulated Annealing and Boltzmann Machines: A Stochastic Approach to Combinatorial Optimization and Neural Computing*. John Wiley, New York.

Anderson, T. W. (1958), *Introduction to Multivariate Statistical Analysis*. John Wiley, New York.

Aoki, Masanao (1974), 'On Some Price Adjustment Schemes'. *Annals of Economic and Social Measurement*, 3:95–115.

Araujo, A. and Sandroni, A. (1992), 'On the Convergence of Bayesian Priors to Rational Expectations in Complete Markets'. Mimeo, IMPA, May.

Arifovic, Jasmina (1991), 'Learning by Genetic Algorithms in Economic Environments'. Ph.D. dissertation, University of Chicago.

_____ (1992a), 'Genetic Algorithm in the Overlapping Generations Economies'. Mimeo, McGill University, June.

_____ (1992b), 'Genetic Algorithm Learning and the Cobweb Model'. Mimeo, McGill University, July.

_____ (1993), 'Genetic Algorithm Learning and Exchange Rate Experiments'. Mimeo, McGill University, May.

Arthur, W. Brian (1989a), 'The Dynamics of Classifier Competitions'. Mimeo, 7 March.

_____ (1989b), 'Nash-Discovering Automata for Finite-Action Games'. Mimeo, Santa Fe Institute.

_____ (1991), 'Designing Economic Agents that Act Like Human Agents: A Behavioral Approach to Bounded Rationality'. *American Economic Review, Papers and Proceedings*, 81:353–9.

Axelrod, Robert (1987), 'The Evolution of Strategies in the Iterated Prisoner's Dilemma'. In Lawrence Davis (ed.), *Genetic Algorithms and Simulated Annealing*. Morgan Kaufman, Los Altos, Calif.

Azariadis, Costas (1981), 'Self-Fulfilling Prophesies'. *Journal of Economic Theory*, 25:380–96.

_____ and Guesnerie, R. (1986), 'Sunspots and Cycles'. *Review of Economic Studies*, 53:725–37.

Barron, A. R. (1991), 'Universal Approximation Bounds for Superpositions of a Sigmoidal Function'. Mimeo, Technical Report no. 58, Department of Statistics, University of Illinois.

Barsalou, Lawrence W. (1992), *Cognitive Psychology: An Overview for Cognitive Scientists*. Lawrence Erlbaum, Hillsdale, NJ.

Beale, R. and Jackson, T. (1990), *Neural Computing: An Introduction*. Adam Hilger, Bristol, Philadelphia, and New York.

Beers, David, Sargent, Thomas, and Wallace, Neil (1983), 'Speculations about the Speculation against the Hong Kong Dollar'. *Federal Reserve Bank of Minneapolis Quarterly Review*, Fall.

Benveniste, Albert, Métivier, Michel, and Priouret, Pierre (1990), *Adaptive Algorithms and Stochastic Approximations*. Springer-Verlag, Berlin and Heidelberg.

Blanchard, Olivier and Watson, Mark (1982), 'Bubbles, Rational Expectations, and Financial Markets'. In Paul Wachtel (ed.), *Crises in the Economic and Financial Structure: Bubbles, Bursts, and Shocks*. Lexington, Mass.: Lexington Books.

Blume, Lawrence and Easley, David (1991a), 'What has the Learning Literature Taught Us?'. Mimeo, Cornell University, June.

_____ _____ (1991b), 'Evolution and Rationality in Competitive Markets'. Mimeo, Cornell University, October.

_____ _____ (1992), 'Rational Expectations and Rational Learning'. Mimeo, Cornell University, June.

Bossaerts, P. (1992), 'Asset Prices in a Speculative Market'. Mimeo, California Institute of Technology.

Boyer, Russell (1971), 'Nickels and Dimes'. Mimeo, University of Western Ontario.

Bray, Margaret M. (1982), 'Learning, Estimation, and Stability of Rational Expectations'. *Journal of Economic Theory*, 26:318–39.

_____ (1983), 'Convergence to Rational Expectations Equilibrium'. In Roman Frydman and Edmund Phelps (eds.), *Individual Forecasts and Aggregate Outcomes*. Cambridge University Press.

_____ and Kreps, David (1987), 'Rational Learning and Rational Expectations'. In George Feiwel (ed.), *Arrow and the Ascent of Modern Economic Theory*. New York University Press, pp. 597–625.

_____ and Savin, N. E. (1986), 'Rational Expectations Equilibria, Learning, and Model Specification'. *Econometrica*, 54:1129–60.

Brock, William A. (1972), 'On Models of Expectations Generated by Maximizing Behavior of Economic Agents Over Time'. *Journal of Economic Theory*, 5:479–513.

_____ (1974), 'Money and Growth: The Case of Long Run Perfect Foresight'. *International Economic Review*, 15:750–77.

_____ (1992), 'Beyond Randomness, or, Emergent Noise: Interactive Systems of Agents with Cross Dependent Characteristics'. Mimeo, Department of Economics, University of Wisconsin, June.

Bruno, Michael and Fischer, Stanley (1990), 'Seigniorage, Operating Rules, and the High Inflation Trap'. *Quarterly Journal of Economics*, 105:353–74.

Bullard, James (1991), 'Learning Equilibria'. Mimeo, Federal Reserve Bank of St. Louis, August.

_____ and Duffy, John (1993), 'Learning in a Large Square Economy'. Mimeo, Federal Reserve Bank of St. Louis, March.

Burns, Arthur M. and Mitchell, Wesley C. (1946), *Measuring Business Cycles*. National Bureau of Economic Research, New York.

Cagan, Phillip (1956), 'The Monetary Dynamics of Hyperinflation'. In Milton Friedman (ed.), *Studies in the Quantity Theory of Money*. University of Chicago Press.

Calvo, Guillermo (1988), 'Passive Money and Idiosyncratic Expectations'. Mimeo, University of Pennsylvania.

Canova, Fabio (1993), 'Modelling and Forecasting Exchange Rates with a Bayesian Time-varying Coefficient Model'. *Journal of Economic Dynamics and Control*, 17:233–61.

Cass, D. and Shell, K. (1983), 'Do Sunspots Matter?'. *Journal of Political Economy*, 91:193–227.

Chen, Xiaohong and White, Halbert (1992), 'Asymptotic Properties of Some Projection-based Robbins-Monro Procedures in a Hilbert Space'. Mimeo, Department of Economics, University of California at San Diego, November.

____ ____ (1993), 'Convergence of Nonparametric Learning Models'. Mimeo, Department of Economics, University of California at San Diego, February.

Cho, In-Koo (1992), 'Perceptrons Play the Repeated Prisoner's Dilemma'. Mimeo, University of Chicago, September.

____ and Matsui, Akihiko (1992), 'Learning and Ramsey Policy'. Mimeo, University of Chicago and University of Pennsylvania, February.

Christiano, Lawrence J. (1987), 'Cagan's Model of Hyperinflation under Rational Expectations'. *International Economic Review*, 28:33–49.

Chung, Heetaik (1990), 'Did Policy Makers Really Believe in the Phillips Curve? An Econometric Test'. Ph.D. dissertation, University of Minnesota, November.

Das, S. R. (1991), 'On the Synthesis of Nonlinear Continuous Neural Networks'. *IEEE Transactions on Systems, Man, and Cybernetics*, 21:413–19.

DeCanio, Stephen J. (1979), 'Rational Expectations and Learning from Experience'. *Quarterly Journal of Economics*, 93:47–57.

Diebold, Francis X. and Nason, James (1990), 'Nonparametric Exchange Rate Prediction?' *Journal of International Economics*, 28:315–32.

Doan, T., Litterman, F., and Sims, C.A. (1984), 'Forecasting and Conditional Projections Using Realistic Prior Distributions'. *Economic Reviews*, 3:1–100.

El-Gamal, Mahmoud A. (1992), 'A Dynamic Migration Model of Uncertainty'. Mimeo, California Institute of Technology, April.

____ and Sundaram, R. K. (1993), 'Bayesian Economists . . . Bayesian Agents: An Alternative Approach to Optimal Learning'. *Journal of Economic Dynamics and Control*, 17:355–83.

Ellison, Glenn and Fudenberg, Drew (1992), 'Rules of Thumb for Social Learning'. Mimeo, June.

Elman, J. L. (1988), 'Finding Structure in Time'. Mimeo, CRL Report 8801, Center for Research in Language, University of California at San Diego.

Evans, George (1983), 'The Stability of Rational Expectations in Macroeconomic Models'. In Roman Frydman and Edmund Phelps (eds.), *Individual Forecasting and Aggregate Outcomes: 'Rational Expectations' Examined*. Cambridge University Press.

____ (1985), 'Expectational Stability and the Multiple Equilibria Problem in Linear Rational Expectations Models'. *Quarterly Journal of Economics*, 100:1217–34.

____ (1989), 'The Fragility of Sunspots and Bubbles'. *Journal of Monetary Economics*, 23:297–313.

____ and Honkapohja, Seppo (1990), 'Learning, Convergence, and Stability with Multiple Rational Expectations Equilibria'. *Working paper*, London School of Economics and Political Science.

____ ____ (1992a), 'Local Convergence of Recursive Learning to Steady States and Cycles in Stochastic Nonlinear Models'. Mimeo, London School of Economics, January.

Evans, George and Honkapohja, Seppo (1992b), 'Adaptive Learning and Expectational Stability: An Introduction'. Mimeo, London School of Economics, March.

—— —— (1992c), 'On the Local Stability of Sunspot Equilibria under Adaptive Learning Rules'. Mimeo, Discussion Paper no. TE/92/249, Suntory-Toyota Workshop, March.

—— —— (1993a), 'Learning and Economic Fluctuations: Using Fiscal Policy to Steer Expectations'. *European Economic Review*, 37:595–602.

—— —— (1993b), 'Adaptive Forecasts, Hysteresis and Endogenous Fluctuations'. *Federal Reserve Bank of San Francisco Review*, in press.

—— —— and Sargent, Thomas J. (1993), 'On the Preservation of Deterministic Cycles when Some Agents Perceive Them to be Deterministic'. *Journal of Economic Dynamics and Control*, in press.

Feldman, Mark (1987), 'An Example of Convergence to Rational Expectations with Heterogeneous Beliefs'. *International Economic Review*, 28:635–50.

Fisher, R. A. (1936), 'The Use of Multiple Measurements in Taxonomic Problems'. *Annals of Eugenics*, 7:179–88.

Flood, Robert P. and Garber, Peter M. (1980), 'An Economic Theory of Monetary Reform'. *Journal of Political Economy*, 88:24–58.

—— —— (1983), 'Process Consistency and Monetary Reform: Some Further Evidence'. *Journal of Monetary Economics*, 12:279–95.

Fourgeaud, C., Gouriéroux, C., and Pradel, J. (1986), 'Learning Procedure and Convergence to Rationality'. *Econometrica*, 54:845–68.

Friedman, Daniel (1991), 'Evolutionary Games in Economics'. *Econometrica*, 59:637–66.

—— and Sunder, Shyam (1992), 'Experimental Methods: A Primer for Economists'. Mimeo, University of California at Santa Cruz.

Friedman, Milton (1953), 'The Methodology of Positive Economics'. In Milton Friedman (ed.), *Essays in Positive Economics*. University of Chicago Press.

—— (1956), *A Theory of the Consumption Function*. Princeton University Press.

—— (1963), 'Windfalls, the 'Horizon,' and Related Concepts in the Permanent-Income Hypothesis'. In Carl Christ *et al.* (eds.), *Measurement in Economics*. Stanford University Press.

—— and Schwartz, Anna (1963), *A Monetary History of the United States*. Princeton University Press.

Futia, Carl A. (1981), 'Rational Expectations in Stationary Linear Models'. *Econometrica*, 49:171–92.

Gale, David (1973), 'Pure Exchange Equilibria of Dynamic Economic Models'. *Journal of Economic Theory*, 6:12–36.

Gallant, A. R., and White, H. (1988), 'There Exists a Neural Network That Does Not Make Avoidable Mistakes'. *IEEE Second International Conference on Neural Networks*, SOS Printing, San Diego, pp. 657–64.

Garber, Peter M. (1982), 'Transition from Inflation to Price Stability'. *Carnegie-Rochester Conference Series on Public Policy*, 16:11–42.

Goldberg, D.E. (1989), *Genetic Algorithms in Search, Optimization, and Machine Learning*. Addison-Wesley, Menlo Park, Calif.

Grandmont, J. M. (1990), 'Expectations Formation and Stability of the Economic System'. Mimeo, Econometric Society Presidential Address.

Gresik, Thomas A., and Satterthwaite, Mark A. (1989), 'The Rate at Which a Simple Market Converges to Efficiency as the Number of Trades Increases: An Asymptotic Result for Optimal Trading Mechanisms'. *Journal of Economic Theory*, 48:304–32.

Hamilton, James D. (1989), 'A New Approach to the Economic Analysis of Nonstationary Time Series and the Business Cycle'. *Econometrica*, 57:357–84.

Hansen, Lars Peter and Sargent, Thomas J. (1983), 'Aggregation over Time and the Inverse Optimal Predictor Problem for Adaptive Expectations in Continuous Time'. *International Economic Review*, 24:1–20.

—— —— (1993), 'Seasonality and Approximation Errors in Rational Expectations Models'. *Journal of Econometrics*, 55:21–55.

Hebb, D.O. (1949), *The Organization of Behavior*. John Wiley, New York.

Hertz, John, Krogh, Anders, and Palmer, Richard (1991), *Introduction to the Theory of Neural Computation*. Addison-Wesley, Redwood City, Calif.

Holland, J. H. (1975), *Adaptation in Natural and Artificial Systems*. University of Michigan Press, Ann Arbor, Mich.

—— (1986), 'Escaping Brittleness: The Possibilities of General-Purpose Learning Algorithms Applied to Parallel Rule-Based Systems'. In R. S. Michalski, J. G. Carbonell, and T. M. Mitchell (eds.), *Machine Learning: An Artificial Intelligence Approach*, ii. Morgan Kaufmann, Los Altos, Calif.

Honkapohja, Seppo (1993), 'Adaptive Learning and Bounded Rationality'. *European Economic Review*, 37:587–94.

Hopfield, J. J. (1982), 'Neural Networks and Physical Systems with Emergent Collective Computational Abilities'. *Proceedings of the National Academy of Science, USA*, 79:2554–8.

Hornik, Kurt, Stinchcombe, Maxell, and White, Halbert (1989), 'Multi-layer Feedforward Networks are Universal Approximators'. Mimeo, Department of Economics, University of California at San Diego, February.

Howitt, Peter (1992), 'Interest Rate Control and Nonconvergence to Rational Expectations'. *Journal of Political Economy*, 100:776–800.

—— and McAfee, R. P. (1988), 'Stability of Equilibria with Externalities'. *Quarterly Journal of Economics*, 103:261–77.

Hurwicz, Leonid (1946), 'Theory of the Firm and of Investment'. *Econometrica*, 14:109–36.

—— (1951), 'Comment'. *Conference on Business Cycles*, National Bureau of Economic Research, New York, pp. 416–20.

Hussman, John (1992), 'Market Efficiency and Inefficiency in Rational Expectations Equilibria'. *Journal of Economic Dynamics and Control*, 16:655–80.

—— and Sargent, Thomas J. (1993), 'Least Squares Learning in a No-Trade Environment'. Mimeo, Hoover Institution.

Imrohoroğlu, Selahattin (1993), 'Testing for Sunspot Equilibria in the German Hyperinflation'. *Journal of Economic Dynamics and Control*, 17:289–318.

Jordan, James S. (1992), 'Convergence to Rational Expectations in a Stationary Linear Game'. *Review of Economic Studies*, 59:109–24.

Jöreskog, K. G. (1967), 'Some Contributions to Maximum Likelihood Factor Analysis'. *Psychometrica*, 32:443–82.

Judd, Kenneth L. (1990), 'Minimum Weighted Residual Methods for Solving Dynamic Economic Models'. Mimeo, Hoover Institution, July.

—— (1992), 'Numerical Methods in Economics'. Mimeo, Hoover Institution, December.

Kandori, M., Mailath, G., and Rob, R. (1992), 'Learning, Mutation, and Long

Run Equilibrium in Games'. Mimeo, University of Pennsylvania.

Kareken, John and Wallace, Neil (1978), 'Deposit Insurance and Bank Regulation: A Partial Equilibrium Exposition'. *Journal of Business*, 51:413–38.

—— —— (1981), 'On the Indeterminacy of Equilibrium Exchange Rates'. *Quarterly Journal of Economics*, 96:207–22.

Kendall, M. G. (1957), *A Course in Multivariate Analysis*. Charles Griffin, London.

Ketterer, J. A. and Marcet, A. (1989), 'Introduction of Derivative Securities: A General Equilibrium Approach'. Mimeo, Carnegie–Mellon University, June.

Kiefer, Nicholas M. (1989), 'A Value Function Arising in the Economics of Information'. *Journal of Economic Dynamics and Control*, 13:201–23.

—— and Nyarko, Yaw (1989), 'Control of an Unknown Linear Process with Learning'. *International Economic Review*, 30:571–86.

—— —— (1991), 'Savage Bayesian Models of Economics'. Mimeo, Cornell University, September.

King, Robert G., Wallace, Neil, and Weber, Warren E. (1992), 'Nonfundamental Uncertainty and Exchange Rates'. *Journal of International Economics*, 32:83–108.

Kiyotaki, Nobuhiro and Wright, Randall (1989), 'On Money as a Medium of Exchange'. *Journal of Political Economy*, 97:927–54.

Kosko, Bart (1992), *Neural Networks and Fuzzy Systems: A Dynamical Approach to Machine Intelligence*. Prentice-Hall, Englewood Cliffs, NJ.

Kreps, David (1990), *Game Theory and Economic Modelling*. Oxford University Press.

Kuan, Chung-Ming (1989), 'Estimation of Neural Network Models'. Ph.D. dissertation, Department of Economics, University of California at San Diego.

—— and White, Halbert (1991), 'Strong Convergence of Recursive M-Estimators for Models with Dynamic Latent Variables'. Mimeo, University of Illinois, March.

—— and Liu, Tung (1991), 'Forecasting Exchange Rates Using Feedforward and Recurrent Neural Networks'. Mimeo, University of Illinois, December.

Kushner, H. J. and Clark, D. S. (1978), *Stochastic Approximation Methods for Constrained and Unconstrained Systems*. Springer-Verlag, New York and Berlin.

Kydland, Finn E. and Prescott, Edward C. (1977), 'Rules Rather Than Discretion: The Inconsistency of Optimal Plans'. *Journal of Political Economy*, 85:473–93.

—— —— (1982), 'Time to Build and Aggregate Fluctuations'. *Econometrica*, 50:1345–70.

LaHaye, Laura (1985), 'Inflation and Currency Reform'. *Journal of Political Economy*, 93:537–60.

Levi, Primo (1984), *The Periodic Table,* trans. Raymond Rosenthal. Schocken Books, New York.

Lim, S. S., Prescott, E. C., and Sunder, S. (1988), 'Stationary Solution to the Overlapping Generations Model of Fiat Money: Experimental Evidence'. Mimeo, University of Minnesota.

Litterman, Robert and Knez, Peter (1989), 'Genetic Algorithm for the Kiyotaki–Wright Model'. Mimeo, Goldman-Sachs.

—— Quah, Danny, and Sargent, Thomas J. (1984), 'Business Cycle Models with Unobservable Index Models and the Method of the NBER'. Mimeo, Federal Reserve Bank of Minneapolis, June.

Ljung, Lennart (1977), 'Analysis of Recursive Stochastic Algorithms'. *IEEE Transactions on Automatic Control*, 22:551–75.

―――― and Söderström, T. (1983), *Theory and Practice of Recursive Identification*. MIT Press, Cambridge, Mass.

―――― Pflug, Georg, and Walk, Harro (1992), *Stochastic Approximation and Optimization of Random Systems*. Birkhäuser Verlag, Basel, Boston, and Berlin.

Lucas, Robert E., Jr. (1972), 'Econometric Testing of the Natural Rate Hypothesis'. In O. Eckstein (ed.), *The Econometrics of Price Determination Conference*. Board of Governors of the Federal Reserve System and Social Science Research Council.

―――― (1983), *Understanding Business Cycles*. MIT Press, Cambridge, Mass.

―――― (1986), 'Adaptive Behavior and Economic Theory'. *Journal of Business*, 59:5401–26.

―――― and Prescott, Edward C. (1971), 'Investment Under Uncertainty'. *Econometrica*, 39:659–81.

Manuelli, Rodolfo E. and Peck, James (1990), 'Exchange Rate Volatility in an Equilibrium Asset Pricing Model'. *International Economic Review*, 31:559–74.

Marcet, Albert (1991), 'Solving Non-Linear Models by Parameterizing Expectations'. Mimeo, Carnegie–Mellon University.

―――― and Marshall, David A. (1992), 'Convergence of Approximate Model Solutions to Rational Expectations Equilibria using the Method of Parameterized Expectations'. Mimeo, Northwestern University, March.

―――― and Sargent, Thomas J. (1989a), 'Convergence of Least Squares Learning Mechanisms in Self Referential Linear Stochastic Models'. *Journal of Economic Theory*, 48:337–68.

―――― ―――― (1989b), 'Convergence of Least Squares Learning in Environments with Hidden State Variables and Private Information'. *Journal of Political Economy*, 97:1306–22.

―――― ―――― (1989c), 'Least Squares Learning and the Dynamics of Hyperinflation'. In William Barnett, John Geweke and Karl Shell (eds.), *Economic Complexity: Chaos, Sunspots, and Nonlinearity*. Cambridge University Press.

―――― ―――― (1992), 'The Convergence of Vector Autoregressions to Rational Expectations Equilibrium'. In Alessandro Vercelli and Nicola Dimitri (eds.), *Macroeconomics: A Strategic Survey*. Oxford University Press.

―――― ―――― (1993), 'Speed of Convergence of Recursive Least Squares Learning with ARMA Perceptions'. In Alan Kirman and Mark Salmon (eds.), *Learning and Rationality in Economics*. Basil Blackwell, Oxford.

Marimon, Ramon and McGrattan, Ellen R. (1993), 'On Adaptive Learning in Strategic Games'. In Alan Kirman and Mark Salmon (eds.), *Learning and Rationality in Economics*. Basil Blackwell, Oxford.

―――― and Sunder, Shyam (1992), 'Indeterminacy of Equilibria in a Hyperinflationary World: Experimental Evidence'. Mimeo, University of Minnesota and Carnegie–Mellon University, August.

―――― McGrattan, E., and Sargent, T. (1990), 'Money as a Medium of Exchange in an Economy with Artificially Intelligent Agents'. *Journal of Economic Dynamics and Control*, 14:329–74.

Maskin, Eric (1991), 'Evolution and Communication in Games'. Mimeo, Harvard University, April.

Matsuyama, Kiminori, Kiyotaki, Nobuhiro, and Matsui, Akihiko (1992), 'Toward a Theory of International Currency'. Mimeo, Hoover Institution,

March.

McKelvey, R. and Palfrey, T. (1992), 'An Experimental Study of the Centipede Game'. *Econometrica*, 60:803–36.

McLennan, Andrew (1984), 'Price Dispersion and Incomplete Learning in the Long-Run'. *Journal of Economic Dynamics and Control*, 7:331–47.

Merton, Robert C (1978), 'On the Cost of Deposit Insurance When There are Surveillance Costs'. *Journal of Business*, 51:439–52.

Milgrom, Paul and Stokey, Nancy (1982), 'Information, Trade, and Common Knowledge'. *Journal of Economic Theory*, 26:17–27.

Minsky, M. L., and Papert, S.A. (1969), *Perceptrons*. MIT Press, Cambridge, Mass.

Mohr, Michael (1990), 'Asymptotic Theory for Least Squares Estimators in Regression Models with Forecast Feedback'. Mimeo, Bonn University.

Moore, Bartholomew J. (1992), 'Least Squares Learning in a Model of Endogenous Growth'. Mimeo, Rutgers University, June.

—— (1993), 'Least Squares Learning and the Stability of Equilibria with Externalities'. *Review of Economic Studies*, 60:197–208.

Müller, Berndt and Reinhardt, Joachim (1990), *Neural Networks: An Introduction*. Springer-Verlag, Berlin and Heidelberg.

Muth, John F. (1960), 'Optimal Properties of Exponentially Weighted Forecasts'. *Journal of the American Statistical Association*, 55:299–306.

—— (1961), 'Rational Expectations and the Theory of Price Movements'. *Econometrica*, 29:315–35.

Nyarko, Yaw (1991), 'On the Convergence of Bayesian Posterior Processes in Linear Economic Models: Counting Equations and Unknowns'. *Journal of Economic Dynamics and Control*, 15:687–713.

—— (1993), 'Learning in Mis-Specified Models and the Possibility of Cycles'. *Journal of Economic Theory*, in press.

—— and Olson, Lars (1991), 'Optimal Growth with Unobservable Resources and Learning'. Mimeo, New York University.

Oja, E. (1982), 'A Simplified Neuron Model as a Principal Component Analyzer'. *Journal of Mathematical Biology*, 15:267–74.

—— and Karhunen, J. (1985), 'On Stochastic Approximation of the Eigenvectors and Eigenvalues of the Expectation of a Random Matrix'. *Journal of Mathematical Analysis and Applications*, 106:69–84.

Pais, Abraham (1992), *Niel Bohr's Times in Physics, Philosophy, and Polity*. Clarendon Press, Oxford and New York.

Peterson, Carsten and Söderberg, Bo (1992), 'Artificial Neural Networks and Combinatorial Optimization Problems'. In E. H. L. Arts and J. K. Lenstra (eds.), *Local Search in Combinatorial Optimization*. John Wiley, New York.

Rissanen, J. (1989), *Stochastic Complexity in Statisical Inquiry*. World Science, Singapore.

Robbins, J. and Monro, S. (1951), 'A Stochastic Approximation Method'. *Annals of Mathematical Statistics*, 22:400–7.

Rosenthal, R. (1981), 'Games of Perfect Information, Predatory Pricing, and the Chain Store Paradox'. *Journal of Economic Theory*, 25:92–100.

Rust, John, Palmer, Richard, and Miller, John H. (1992), 'Behavior of Trading Automata in a Computerized Double Auction Market'. Mimeo, Santa Fe Institute, January.

Samuelson, Paul (1958), 'An Exact Consumption-Loan Model with or without the Social Contrivance of Money'. *Journal of Political Economy*, 66:467–82.

Sargent, Thomas J. (1971), 'A Note on the Accelerationist Controversy'. *Journal of Money, Credit, and Banking*, 8:721–5.

—— (1977), 'The Demand for Money during Hyperinflations under Rational Expectations: I'. *International Economic Review*, 18:59–82.

—— (1986), *Rational Expectations and Inflation*. Harper & Row, New York.

—— (1987), *Macroeconomic Theory*. Academic Press, New York.

—— (1991), 'Equilibrium with Signal Extraction from Endogenous Variables'. *Journal of Economic Dynamics and Control*, 15:245–74.

—— and Sims, Christopher A. (1977), 'Business Cycle Models without Pretending to Have Too Much A Priori Theory'. In Christopher A. Sims (ed.), *Federal Reserve Bank of Minneapolis*. pp. 45–110.

—— and Wallace, Neil (1973), 'Rational Expectations and the Dynamics of Hyperinflation'. *International Economic Review*, 63:328–50.

—— —— (1982), 'The Real Bills Doctrine vs. the Quantity Theory: a Reconsideration'. *Journal of Political Economy*, 90:1212–36.

Schwarz, G. (1978), 'Estimating the Dimension of a Model'. *Annals of Statistics*, 6:461–4.

Simon, Herbert A. (1957), *Models of Man: Social and Rational; Mathematical Essays on Rational Human Behavior in Society Setting*. John Wiley, New York.

Sims, Christopher A. (1972), 'Approximate Prior Restrictions in Distributed Lag Estimation'. *Journal of the American Statistical Association*, 67:169–75.

—— (1980), 'Macroeconomics and Reality'. *Econometrica*, 69:1–48.

—— (1988), 'Projecting Policy Effects with Statistical Models'. *Revista de Analisis Economico*, 3:3–20.

Singleton, Kenneth J. (1987), 'Asset Prices in a Time Series Model with Disparately Informed, Competitive Traders'. In William A. Barnett and Kenneth J. Singleton (eds.), *New Approaches to Monetary Economics*. Cambridge University Press.

Smith, Bruce C. (1988), 'Legal Restrictions, "Sunspots," and Peel's Bank Act: The Real Bills Doctrine versus the Quantity Theory Reconsidered'. *Journal of Political Economy*, 96:3–19.

Smith, John Maynard (1982), *Evolution and the Theory of Games*. Cambridge University Press.

Swinkels, Jeroen M. (1992), 'Adjustment Dynamics and Rational Play in Games'. Mimeo, Department of Economics, Stanford University, July.

Taylor, John (1975), 'Monetary Policy during a Transition to Rational Expectations'. *Journal of Political Economy*, 83:1009–21.

Tirole, Jean (1982), 'On the Possibility of Speculation under Rational Expectations'. *Econometrica*, 50:1163–81.

Townsend, R. M. (1983), 'Forecasting the Forecasts of Others'. *Journal of Political Economy*, 91:546–88.

Uhlig, Harald (1992), 'Costly Information Acquisition, Stock Prices and Neoclassical Growth'. Mimeo, Princeton University, March.

Vives, X. (1992), 'How Fast Do Rational Agents Learn?'. Mimeo, Institut d'Anàlisi Econòmica, Universitat Autònoma de Barcelona.

Wallace, Neil (1980), 'The Overlapping-Generations Model of Fiat Money'. In J. H. Kareken and N. Wallace (eds.), *Models of Monetary Economies*. Minneapolis: Federal Reserve Bank of Minneapolis, pp. 49–82.

Wang, Jiang (1990), 'A Model of Intertemporal Asset Prices under Asymmetric Information'. Mimeo, Massachusetts Institute of Technology.

White, Halbert (1982), 'Maximum Likelihood Estimation of Misspecified Models'. *Econometrica*, 50:1–26.

———— (1988), 'Economic Prediction Using Neural Networks: The Case of IBM Stock Prices'. *Proceedings of the IEEE Second International Conference on Neural Networks*, ii:451–8.

Woodford, Michael (1990), 'Learning to Believe in Sunspots'. *Econometrica*, 58:277–307.

Wright, Randall (1993), 'Search, Evolution, and Money'. *Journal of Economic Dynamics and Control*, in press.

Young, H. Peyton (1991), 'Conventional Equilibria'. Mimeo, University of Maryland, June.

Author Index

Author Index

Subject Index